THE WHAT,

WHY AND

HOW OF
ASSESSMENT

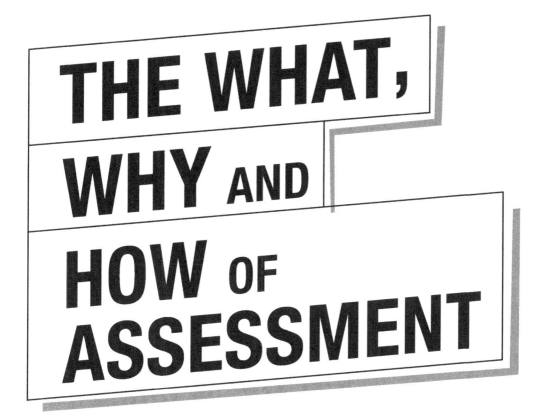

THE WHAT, WHY AND HOW OF ASSESSMENT

A GUIDE FOR TEACHERS AND SCHOOL LEADERS

SIMON CHILD
PAUL ELLIS

CORWIN

A SAGE company
2455 Teller Road
Thousand Oaks, California 91320
(0800)233-9936
www.corwin.com

SAGE Publications Ltd
1 Oliver's Yard
55 City Road
London EC1Y 1SP

SAGE Publications India Pvt Ltd
B 1/I 1 Mohan Cooperative Industrial Area
Mathura Road
New Delhi 110 044

SAGE Publications Asia-Pacific Pte Ltd
3 Church Street
#10-04 Samsung Hub
Singapore 049483

© 2021 Simon Child and Paul Ellis

First published in 2021

Editor: Amy Thornton
Senior project editor: Chris Marke
Marketing manager: Dilhara Attygalle
Cover design: Wendy Scott
Typeset by: C&M Digitals (P) Ltd, Chennai, India
Printed in the UK

Library of Congress Control Number 2021936816

British Library Cataloguing in Publication Data

A catalogue record for this book is available from the British Library

ISBN 978-1-5297-5255-7
ISBN 978-1-5297-5254-0 (pbk)

At SAGE we take sustainability seriously. Most of our products are printed in the UK using responsibly sourced papers and boards. When we print overseas we ensure sustainable papers are used as measured by the PREPS grading system. We undertake an annual audit to monitor our sustainability.

CONTENTS

FIGURES AND TABLES

FIGURES

TABLES

ABOUT THE AUTHORS

 **Simon Child** is Head of Assessment Training at the Cambridge Assessment Network, and the co-course director for the Postgraduate Advanced Certificate in Educational Studies: Educational Assessment at the University of Cambridge. Previously, he was a Principal Research Officer in the Assessment Research and Development Division of Cambridge Assessment. He has conducted research in the field of qualifications reform and development since 2012.

His research interests include quality of marking processes, curriculum development, formative assessment and the assessment of '21st-century skills'. His background is in developmental psychology. In 2011, he received his PhD from the University of Manchester, which focused on the development of symbolic cognition in preschool children.

 **Paul Ellis** is Head of Teaching and Learning at Cambridge Assessment International Education. He began teaching in schools and universities in the 1990s, and – having also worked at the International Baccalaureate organisation – has held senior positions in two of the main global education providers since 2006. In his current role, he works with teachers and school leaders worldwide to advise and support them in their professional learning.

His specialisms include language education, music, neurodiversity, mental health and well-being. He broadcasts widely on aspects of teaching and learning at conferences, through webinars, workshops, podcasts and blogs. He has co-authored or edited more than a dozen education books, including *The Trainer Toolkit: A Guide to Delivering Training in Schools* (Corwin, 2020).

FOREWORD BY TIM OATES CBE

In the early 2000s I felt it was important to broaden the way we thought about assessment. I enjoy convening conferences and seminars. Constructed carefully, they can make significant contributions to thought and action. I began to put together the outline of a conference where we would bring together leading historians, economists, anthropologists and sociologists to begin to unpack all the influences and pressures on assessment – to provide a more complete picture of the place of assessment and the way that it's developed and possible future directions. But one thing stood in the way. Not one of these people, each pre-eminent in their field, felt that they were qualified to even begin to think about qualifications and assessment. "No... not possible..."; "...I can't think of a way my discipline can contribute..." What emerged from the telephone calls and discussions was a sense of assessment being totally alien and intimidating – a highly technical field which other disciplines had no overlap with, no points of engagement.

I was disappointed, but understood why. The experience confirmed the way in which assessment and qualifications are somehow seen as remote and technical. The security surrounding traditional unseen exams perhaps contributes. And the mystery of how answers on exam papers go back to an exam board or assessment organisation and grades, sometime later, return. And the idea that 'knowing the detail' might be a form of 'cheating' – of 'playing the system'. I worked with officials in the 1990s who did not want the lid to be lifted on examination processes, who wanted to maintain arrangements as 'closed internal processes' – even at the time that the nation was experimenting with school-devised exams and various forms of continuous, teacher-based assessment. In all of this there's an enduring ambiguity as to who 'owns' assessment and qualifications: The State? Exam boards and agencies? The users? Schools and learners? Society?

Just as greater transparency permeates social, economic and political life, and 'taking responsibility' and 'personal agency' become ever-present assumptions, the world of assessment and qualifications remains a relatively closed one. Opening up the 'closed and inaccessible workings', allowing others to understand processes, turning the arcane into the accessible – that's what this book is about. In widening understanding, in making knowledge public, there is a chance of improving learning, enhancing the use of information from assessment, and ensuring that public views enter the world of assessment policy. Assessment and qualifications can, and should be, a 'shared public institution' – something which supports enduring, high-quality and ever-improving processes. This book is a fundamental contribution to achieving this.

Tim Oates CBE

Group Director, Assessment Research and Development, Cambridge University Press & Cambridge Assessment

INTRODUCTION

Assessment is something that we all encounter throughout our lives. For teachers, school leaders, other educators and those with responsibility for educational policy, a sound understanding of the principles and practices of assessment is fundamental for effective teaching and learning to take place. The more 'assessment-literate' we become, the more able we are to effect positive change for our students and obtain evidence to inform how we improve what we do. Assessment literacy also enables educators to have the tools to innovate in their practice, and in turn contribute to broader educational outcomes.

The importance of assessment literacy is illustrated by the emphasis given to related competencies in a range of professional standards frameworks for teachers, including the early career framework[1] and the professional standards for teaching and leadership[2] in the UK. However, while the need for professional development in assessment is high, knowledge of and confidence around assessment issues is generally low.[3]

I feel confident that I ...	0	1	2	3
1 ... can describe different purposes of assessment that are relevant to my practice.				
2 ... can demonstrate an understanding of the relationship between the key principles in educational assessment.				
3 ... know how an examination paper is created by an assessment organisation.				
4 ... know how marking and grading are administered in an assessment organisation.				
5 ... know why and how assessments are standardised and moderated.				
6 ... can interpret and use assessment data effectively.				
7 ... understand why it is hard to assess concepts such as community action and service, collaborative work, and the expressive arts.				
8 ... know how to prepare students effectively for assessment.				
9 ... can support mental health and well-being issues related to assessment.				
10 ... consider the extent to which educational assessments are inclusive in their design.				
11 ... can contribute to the debate about how assessments might evolve in the future.				
12 ... can describe key concepts in educational assessment to others.				

This is why we have written this book. Our aim is to guide you through the key principles of assessment, to demonstrate them in action, and to show how assessment can be designed to set learners up for success. This book will give you opportunities to reflect on your own approaches to assessment with teaching and learning in mind, with an emphasis on equipping you to be a confident assessment practitioner.

Before we begin, here is a short questionnaire for you to think about your own knowledge, understanding and confidence in using assessment in your professional context. Consider each statement in turn and rate yourself honestly against each – the higher the number, the more confident you feel. As you go through this book, you can reflect on these statements and your initial ratings.

HOW TO USE THIS BOOK

We have divided the book into three sections. **Part A** focuses on the principles of assessment, exploring its definitions and purposes, and then taking you in turn through the key concepts of validity, reliability, fairness and standards. **Part B** illustrates these principles in action, beginning with an exploration of how examination papers are created and marked in an assessment organisation. We then look at how assessment is used in schools, including the data that are generated from it. This part concludes with a discussion of the challenges of assessing specific types of activity and areas of the curriculum.

In **Part C**, we discuss how different educational approaches can support students and other assessment-takers to be successful. We start with a consideration of how assessment can be integrated with teaching and learning to get students ready for examinations at the end of their studies. We then take a close look at mental health and well-being with reference to test anxiety, before evaluating what can be done to make assessment more accessible and inclusive. In the final chapter, we explore the arguments for change in assessment methodology and how assessment could evolve.

In each chapter, we have included a range of inset boxes. These can be used as 'pauses for thought' for individual readers or as part of group discussions in continued professional development (CPD) sessions. There are three types of box:

 Reflection: These are activities that invite you to consider ideas introduced in a chapter. They aim to connect theoretical perspectives with your own practice.

 Practical: These 'hands-on' boxes give specific advice on how to create effective and valid assessments.

 Extension: These boxes introduce more complex ideas to the chapter, particularly looking at technical and research debates raging in the world of assessment.

To help you navigate, each chapter begins with a brief summary of what you will learn and finishes with a list of key takeaways. We recommend that you choose your own route through the book: it is not intended to be linear, but later chapters often reference ideas introduced earlier in the book. This approach offers an opportunity for readers to use the book flexibly and reflects the interconnected nature of many of the ideas introduced in individual chapters. Some words or phrases, shown in bold in the text, are defined in the **Glossary**.

The book is a result of our own knowledge and experience from working in the field of professional development of teachers and school leaders. We have drawn upon the research and writing of many other experts in education and assessment, as well as summarising their findings for you in a digestible form. We would like to thank our colleagues and friends in Cambridge and around the world who have supported us in the writing of these chapters. We provide a comprehensive list of references for each chapter at the end of the book. If there are any errors or omissions the publishers would be grateful to be notified of any corrections that should be incorporated in the next edition or reprint of this book.

By reading this book, you will gain a sound understanding of the what, why and how of assessment; feel more confident in your ability to participate in decisions about what works in education; and think about what innovations you can introduce in your professional life. Above all, you will be better equipped to know how we can enable learners to fulfil and demonstrate their potential.

PART A
PRINCIPLES OF ASSESSMENT

1

WHAT IS ASSESSMENT?

IN THIS CHAPTER, YOU WILL:

- learn how 'assessment' and 'educational assessment' can be defined;
- develop understanding of the key properties of educational assessment;
- reflect on the potential purposes of assessment, and how they are different from one another.

A defining characteristic of humans is that they are naturally curious. Curiosity relates to ideas of exploration, investigation, learning and discovery. It is impossible to think of society being so advanced if it was not for the curiosity and innovations of its pioneers across time, including scientists, engineers, mathematicians, designers, musicians and artists. Our curiosity related to others leads us to want to know more about people we live and work with; and to do this, an assessment of one type or another is often used.

Imagine a student sat quiet and still at their desk. You have never seen them before, but you have been tasked with deciding whether this student understands a key concept in mathematics that is crucial for them to know before they go to university. You know that their final end-of-schooling examination is due in about a month, and that it will determine whether they will be permitted to enter university. How do you go about finding a window into this student's mind? The answer will be, in one sense or another, an assessment.

In **Part A**, we cover some of the fundamental principles in educational assessment, including validity, reliability, fairness and standards. Before we begin exploring each of these interrelated concepts in turn, it is important to understand the 'what' and 'why' of assessment. In this chapter, we explain assessment as being the process of collecting and interpreting evidence that is put to some use by practitioners with respect to a specific purpose (or purposes). We also describe that assessment involves elements of both measurement and human judgement.

ASSESSMENT IS THE PROCESS OF COLLECTING AND INTERPRETING EVIDENCE

Put in its simplest terms, 'assessment' is the process of collecting evidence with respect to something that we want to know more about. In the modern world, assessment is used every day to help guide decisions taken in daily life. For example, if you visit a doctor's surgery with a medical issue, the doctor will ask you a series of questions concerning your particular complaint, gathering evidence to gradually exclude different possibilities until a prospective diagnosis can be made. These questions may be supported by further measurements (e.g. blood pressure) that guide the doctor in their decision-making.

'Educational assessment' is the process of gathering and recording evidence about a learner's response to a planned task. In the planning of the task, the assessor needs to have an in-depth understanding of:

1. what it is that they are interested in knowing more about (known as the **construct**);
2. how best to elicit evidence in relation to the construct; and
3. how to process the information gathered in the best way.

Traditional models of education placed assessment at the end of a teaching and learning experience. 'Assessment *of* learning' is still prevalent, particularly in high-stakes contexts. However, in more recent history, particularly since the publication of Paul Black and Dylan Wiliam's work *Inside the Black Box*,[1] assessment has been incorporated into the teaching and learning experience – what has been termed 'assessment *for* learning' or 'assessment *as* learning'.

The idea of 'assessment *for* learning' emerged from a realisation that assessment cannot be separated from teaching or instruction. Assessment evidence is used to adapt the next instructional steps and helps to organise classroom activity by acting as a key resource to structure learning. Assessment, for example, can help teachers to make inferences about the causes of learner errors. Errors could be from learners holding a misconception or a naive view, or a lack of conceptual or procedural knowledge.[2] From here, teachers can plan the next learning intervention: what Black and Wiliam call the 'moment of contingency'.[3] In **Chapter 12**, we will explore the relationship between these concepts in more detail.

WE PUT THE EVIDENCE THAT WE HAVE COLLATED FROM ASSESSMENT TO A *USE*

Assessment is not delivered in isolation from the educational environment within which it resides. Practitioners usually have an underpinning motivation for why they are using an assessment at a particular time. This may be either to inform a judgement or to help them make an educational decision.

The key point here is that assessment makes it possible for a practitioner to adjust their interactions with learners. Examples might include a teacher deciding to focus their teaching on an identified misconception in mathematics, or an examiner deciding a final grade for a qualification. Assessment in this way can be thought of as a tool that can inform and shape educational practice. Of course, how the information is gathered, recorded and subsequently used can vary in terms of quality and the types of tasks used. There is (in theory at least) a universe of potential constructs that an educator may be interested in, and a wide variety of 'tools' with which to assess them. The quality of an assessment is therefore reliant on practitioners selecting the most optimal methods that elicit the most appropriate evidence.

Let's consider some examples related to the assessment *of* and *for* learning. With 'assessment *of* learning', approaches can often be planned in advance. For instance, imagine that you were interested in assessing students' practical abilities in the sciences. You want to know which students have sufficient competence in practical science so that they can enter a university laboratory safely and with the required understanding of scientific principles and notation. You may have four different options for your planned assessment (see Table 1.1).

Table 1.1   Options for the assessment of practical science knowledge, understanding and skills

Assessment type	Description
Practical examination	A set practical task that is completed and reported upon under examination conditions.
Controlled assessment	A practical task given to teachers beforehand, and then given to students at a later date under examination conditions.
Coursework	A practical task conducted during class time and written up in class or as homework.
Practical activities with supporting examination	Students are given a range of practical activities during the course and asked questions about them during a written examination. Teachers also check student competence during lab-based practical activities conducted during the course.

Which of these models or assessment 'tools' do you think would be most likely to produce the best evidence of the abilities that you are most interested in? Let us briefly explore each option below.

A *practical examination* might be appealing because of the certainty that whatever is produced by each student is their own work, and there is a sense of equity that all of the students have the same opportunity to show what they know. However, there are issues of scalability for this assessment, which may mean that the task set might become predictable over time. For example, limitations in terms of equipment and laboratory space available to schools hosting the practical examination may mean that only a small set of potential practical tasks are accessible to all schools.

Controlled assessment relies on the teacher understanding beforehand what the task is so that they can make the relevant equipment available to students. This introduces the possibility of the teacher coaching students in anticipation of the controlled assessment task.

Coursework has the advantage of reducing examination anxiety, which potentially increases fairness. There is, however, an obvious security issue – how do you know that the work produced is the student's own?

The *practical activities with supporting examination* approach has the advantage that the written work is produced under examination conditions, as well as encouraging teachers to increase students' experiences with many practical activities. However, there is a requirement to check that only students who have had the practical experience are able to answer the items in the examination.

In the domain of 'assessment *for* learning', the evidence collated from assessment activities can either be planned or used in a much more on-the-fly fashion, as part of the interaction between teacher and students. Compared with the use of 'assessment *of* learning', the use of assessment for formative purposes focuses on the direct link between assessment information and how it is used to facilitate learner development, such as through the use of feedback. The practitioner uses assessment evidence to develop a working hypothesis about what learners know and bases their instruction on this information.

In summary, these examples illustrate that assessment is a highly flexible, Swiss Army-like 'tool' for collecting and interpreting evidence. So far, we have sliced the uses for assessment into two broad categories with some illustrative examples. But what other purposes can we have for assessment?

ASSESSMENT CAN HAVE MANY PURPOSES

In the early stages of assessment development, we need to consider an important initial question: Why does a particular assessment need to exist? Above, we have broadly separated assessment according to two categories of use: to summarise learning or to inform learning. This distinction is an important first step in determining what the *purpose* of an assessment is, and to which uses it is going to be put.

The purpose of an assessment should be more detailed than 'to collect evidence' and more specific than 'to keep the classroom quiet for 15 minutes'. Ideally, assessment should focus on the decision or action that the assessment affords which otherwise would not be possible.

Paul Newton, now at the **Office of Qualifications and Examinations Regulation (Ofqual)** in the UK, identified 18 different purposes of educational assessment (see Table 1.2).[4] What is key to this list of purposes is that they all implicate a decision or action which is to be taken by the assessor on the basis of the evidence produced by learners.

Take the example of the student sitting at their desk from the beginning of this chapter. At one level, we have stated a purpose: we would like to know about their understanding of a key mathematical concept *in order to use* that information to guide a teaching decision (e.g. whether they need further instruction on that topic). In other words, we have a *formative* or potentially *diagnostic* purpose.

However, what if your assessment was also used to make a judgement on your abilities as a teacher? In this case, the student's performance reflects on your performance.

Table 1.2 Purposes of educational assessment

Purpose	Description of purpose
Comparability	Aggregated results from earlier assessments are used to compare with the standards for later assessments.
Diagnosis	Identify learning issues or difficulties.
Formative	Identifying learner needs and to direct teaching.
Guidance	Outcomes used to offer direction for learners in terms of their next stage of learning or work.
Institution monitoring	Decide the standards of an educational institution relative to their own history, or that of other institutions.
Licensing	Determine a licence to practise (e.g. as a medical practitioner).
National accounting	Analyse educational performance at a national level.
Organisational intervention	Identify issues in educational institutions and justify intervention.
Placement	Place students in learning groups (e.g. class settings).
Programme evaluation	Evaluate the success of educational programmes.
Qualification	Judge whether a learner has the sufficient knowledge, skills and/or understanding to qualify for a particular position (e.g. a job, a place at university).
Resource allocation	Identify needs and subsequent allocation of resources.
School choice	Deduce the desirability of schools or other educational institutions.
Selection	Predict which applicants are most likely to succeed in a job or a course of instruction.
Social evaluation	Evaluate the social value of personal educational achievements.
Student monitoring	Decide whether learners are making sufficient progress in attainment over time.
System monitoring	Evaluate whether educational standards are moving up or down over time.
Transfer	Tailor educational interventions for learners who have entered a new institution.

This use introduces additional purposes such as *resource allocation, system monitoring, institution monitoring* and *programme evaluation*. These additional purposes will have implications for how the evidence from the assessment should be collected, analysed and processed.

Having multiple purposes for a single assessment or qualification outcome is a common phenomenon in education. Judgements made concerning students are aggregated at the school or national level to make further judgements about the current state of education, as well as setting further targets. Assessment outcomes therefore become a key component of the discourse about the quality of educational institutions and systems.

If a measure becomes a target, however, then it can undermine the original purpose by ceasing to be a sufficiently good measure – this is known as Goodhart's law.[5] In education, some schools have been accused of narrowing the curriculum and teaching only what is in the assessments that contribute to their accountability measurements. For example, in the US, it has been argued that the introduction of **No Child Left Behind** led to a lowering of the standards required for students to be classed as proficient, in addition to an increase in class time being dedicated to the tested subjects of reading, writing and mathematics.[6] The argument here is that although test score performance may have risen in these subject areas, overall educational standards may not have (for a definition of different types of standards, see **Chapter 5**).

REFLECTION

While educational assessments are often designed with one purpose in mind (e.g. measuring academic ability), there is often a requirement for the same assessment to have secondary purposes (e.g. school-level accountability). There is an argument that assessments should have one main purpose, what Paul Newton has called purpose *purism*.[7] There may be additional purposes, he argues, but they should not detract from or undermine the main purpose. The argument behind this position is that purpose-driven assessment design becomes unwieldy and complicated when there are multiple uses for the same assessment.

There is another argument that it is neither time- nor cost-effective to use an assessment for just one purpose; they should have multiple purposes, provided they can all be met. Newton called this purpose *pluralism*.

- Think of an assessment that you know well. Has it been used for more than one purpose? You may want to use Table 1.2 to guide your thinking.
- If so, were any purposes prioritised over others in the design of the assessment?

ASSESSMENT HAS BOTH PROPERTIES OF MEASUREMENT AND JUDGEMENT

At the time of writing, the next Olympic Games due to take place in Tokyo has 33 sports scheduled. For each of these sports, Olympians compete against each other, either directly or indirectly, until the top three (or in some cases four) competitors have been decided upon. The criteria to decide the medallists for each competition vary considerably and have evolved over the course of each sport's unique history and international regulations.

Take, for example, the long jump. For this event, athletes are given a set number of attempts to push with one foot into the air and land as far as possible from a marked plasticine line. Following a legal jump, a measurement is taken from the plasticine line to the closest mark left after landing. The winner of the gold medal is the athlete who has been *measured* as jumping the furthest distance.

In contrast, high diving events employ a judgement system. For each dive, competitors are scored by a panel of seven judges who rate each dive between the scores of 0 and 10. The top two and the bottom two scores are discarded, and then the remaining three scores are added together and multiplied by the dive's *degree of difficulty* rating. The degree of difficulty is calculated according to a formula decided upon by the Fédération Internationale de Natation (FINA). The judges consider four main criteria: the approach and starting position, the take-off from the platform or springboard, the flight through the air, and the entry into the water. The winner of the gold medal is the athlete who has been *judged* to have scored the highest aggregated points following their set of dives.

In educational assessment, measurement and judgement have been placed on two ends of a spectrum, with certain assessment methods argued as having properties of measurement (e.g. multiple-choice questions) and others having properties of judgement (e.g. extended-response essays). However, even the most standardised and validated psychometric tests have a human element to them. At various points in the development of such tests, there will have been judgements made by practitioners, including at the **item** writing stage, during item testing, and when deciding upon a finalised version. The idea of a measurement-to-judgement continuum is therefore not truly applicable in educational assessment; wherever you find assessment, you will find it underpinned by human judgement at some stage of the process.

FINAL THOUGHTS

Assessment practitioners implicitly make decisions by considering several assessment concepts simultaneously, including validity, reliability, fairness and standards. As you progress through this book, you will notice that these principles of good assessment can be applied across different educational scenarios, need to be considered simultaneously, and are often in tension with one another.

In the next chapter, we will look in more detail at the concepts of validity and validation. Validity is a fundamental concept because it concerns the degree of alignment between the purposes of assessment discussed above, the evidence collected from assessment, and the processing of that evidence. Validation concerns evidence to support or refute the claims that we want to make about assessment-takers on the basis of their assessment outcomes. For example, what evidence is there to support the claim that an A-grade student on a mathematics assessment is stronger in terms of mathematical ability compared to a B-grade student? When the stakes are high, we need to think carefully about how we can use qualitative and quantitative evidence to support how we use assessment.

While reliability, fairness and standards are all crucial to good assessment practice, they all support a case for validity. Validity is therefore the assessment concept that rules them all!

KEY TAKEAWAYS

- Assessment is all around us and is fundamentally a means from which to collect evidence related to something that we are interested in knowing more about. This evidence is put to a use by practitioners, typically to inform a decision or to form a judgement.
- Assessment can have either one or multiple purposes.
- Assessment, at some level or another, involves human judgement.

2

VALIDITY

ONE ASSESSMENT CONCEPT TO RULE THEM ALL

IN THIS CHAPTER, YOU WILL:

- learn about key assessment terms, including 'validity', 'validation' and 'construct';
- develop awareness of the different types of validity that are important to assessment practice;
- reflect on how connections are made between constructs and assessment tasks;
- be introduced to a framework for understanding how to validate your assessments.

Many people reading this will have had the nerve-racking experience of a first date. In some cases, particularly in the era of online dating, your prospective partner might have described themselves as 'intelligent', 'interesting' or 'witty'. You will have your own ideas about whether these are things that you are attracted to; but if you are interested in intelligence, for example, one intention of your first date is to establish whether this claim has an element of truth. Implicitly (and perhaps while avoiding talking with your mouth full), you will use the natural flow of conversation to collate and interpret whether this desired characteristic exists in your partner for the evening. But how do you know that the conversation you are engaging in is really establishing the intelligence of your date?

Although it is unlikely that you would ever use them in a dating scenario, you will be familiar with assessments which aim to measure the trait of 'intelligence'. Traits are abstract concepts that are not directly measurable, but developers of intelligence tests have designed and refined a set of items from which they are able to measure the *construct* of intelligence. A construct is a proposed attribute of a person that can be assessed using different sources of evidence. Constructs are therefore a set of observable and definable behaviours that closely align with a proposed trait. In educational assessment, we are interested in establishing how well the design and processes of collecting evidence inform the educational decisions or judgements that we want to make. This is where the concepts of validity and validation become so important for education practitioners to understand.

It is very easy to go down the metaphorical rabbit hole when it comes to validity theory and validation practice. Many eyes glaze over and much of the literature is rather impenetrable. What we hope that you take from this chapter is an understanding of why validity is important to always keep in mind when developing and using assessments. This chapter also aims to help you form a common language for thinking about the validity of your assessments, as well as understanding how you can seek validity evidence appropriately.

VALIDITY IS ABOUT THE INTERPRETATION AND USE OF ASSESSMENT SCORES

Perhaps the best-known definition of validity is given by Samuel Messick, who stated that validity is:

> an integrated evaluative judgement of the *degree to which empirical evidence and theoretical rationales* support the *adequacy and appropriateness of inferences and actions* based on *test scores* or other modes of assessment.[1] [emphasis added]

The emphasised parts of this definition require a little explanation:

Degree to which empirical evidence and theoretical rationales: You might hear people make statements such as 'the assessment is valid' which imply that validity is something which an assessment either does or does not have. This black-and-white conceptualisation of validity is rejected by Messick, as he suggests that an assessment is not directly quantifiable enough to pass such a judgement. Practitioners therefore have a semblance of control over assessment validation; they can collect and evaluate various sources of data to determine whether they can be confident in their assessments.

Adequacy and appropriateness of inferences and actions: This is based on the idea that no assessment is independent of the uses for which it was designed (see **Chapter 1**). The outcomes of the assessment (e.g. the mark achieved or the judgement made about a learner) are used in some way, and so Messick argues that it is important to consider to what extent the inferences we make based on assessment outcomes can be trusted. It is also necessary that the actions which follow an assessment are appropriate. For example, it would not be appropriate to infer from an assessment of mathematics that a student should be selected for a later course in fine arts.[2]

Test scores: These refer to the overall outcome of the assessment, typically a mark or a grade. The label of a mark or a grade leads to a particular inference about a learner, such as about their ability relative to other learners. It might also result in access to the next stage of learning, such as a university course.

Breaking down Messick's classic definition, we can see that validity cannot simply be reduced to the idea that an assessment 'measures what it claims to measure'. Instead, validity judgements revolve around inferences drawn from the assessment and the subsequent actions that result from analysing assessment outcomes. As a result, it is the responsibility of not just assessment developers, but also assessment users such as teachers, students and employers, to consider the validity of assessments with stated purposes.

THERE ARE DIFFERENT TYPES OF VALIDITY IN ASSESSMENT

The title of this chapter suggests that validity is one concept which can be defined, analysed and applied. Unfortunately, it is not quite as simple as that! Over years of research and theoretical wrangling, authors have arrived at several different 'types' of validity. In Table 2.1, we explain some of these validity types and how they are connected.

Table 2.1   Definitions of different types of validity

Validity type	Explanation
Construct validity	The degree to which the assessment that you have created assesses the abilities which are the focus of the course or curriculum. Construct validity therefore relies on a sound description of the construct that you are interested in and a clear understanding of how it is being measured.
Content validity	How closely the content and coverage of the assessment matches the content and coverage of the curriculum, syllabus or specification it is designed to assess. In order to have sufficient content validity, the assessment must cover all relevant parts of the subject that it intends to measure. If a teacher is looking to design an assessment that focuses on students' abilities to transform fractions into decimals, the assessment itself will have a reduced content validity if some types of transformation are left out.
Consequential validity	The extent to which assessment outcomes can be relied on to make sound decisions about learners' abilities. It may also refer to the social consequences that result from using an assessment for a particular purpose. The social consequences of an assessment can be both positive and negative. Positive social consequences might relate to the adapted nature of teaching and instruction that might occur from good-quality assessment, while negative consequences could relate to the psychological impact of assessment on students.
Predictive validity	The extent to which assessment results can be used to predict future behaviour or achievement. Predictive validity becomes important when the purpose of a particular assessment is to differentiate among students for selection. A common example of this is when an end-of-schooling examination is used as part of the selection process for university places or to select people for a job role.
Concurrent validity	How closely the assessment outcomes match the outcomes from similar tests designed to test related achievement or performance. Concurrent validity explores the relationship between two assessments that have been administered at approximately the same time. For example, an assessment related to competency for a job role could be administered, and the scores on this assessment could then be explored in relation to the report rating given in the same week by line managers.

The five types of validity in Table 2.1 have a degree of hierarchy, with content, consequential, predictive and concurrent validity all contributing to the overall construct validity. *Construct validity* is therefore our 'one concept to rule them all'. Furthermore, predictive and concurrent validity come under the single category of what is known as *criterion validity*. Criterion validity is a measure of how well one assessment predicts the outcomes of another assessment.

PRACTICAL BOX 2.1

THE LOGIC OF ASSESSMENT TASK DEVELOPMENT

A difficult aspect of assessment practice is making the connection between seemingly quite abstract ideas related to a trait of interest (e.g. mathematical ability), how that is represented by the construct (e.g. knowledge, skills and understanding that are manifest in particular behaviours), and subsequently how assessment tasks link to the defined construct. In Figure 2.1, there is an overview of this 'logic' of assessment task development.

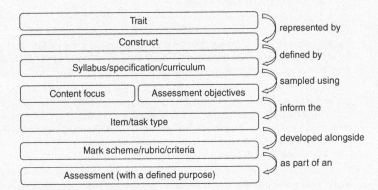

Figure 2.1   The logic of assessment task development

You can see here that there is a gradual 'flow' from more abstract notions of 'trait' and 'construct' to more practical and operational concerns such as assessment task design.

Let us consider an example briefly – the subject of geography. In England, the purpose statement in the national curriculum gives a broad definition of the outcomes of an education in geography up to the end of **Key Stage 3**. A short excerpt is given below:

A high-quality geography education ... should equip pupils with knowledge about diverse places, people, resources and natural and human environments, together with a deep understanding of the Earth's key physical and human processes. As pupils progress, their growing knowledge about the world should help them to deepen their understanding of the interaction between physical and human processes, and of the formation and use of landscapes and environments.[3]

This statement is an indication of the scope and range of topics that need to be covered in an assessment of geography – in other words, the construct. It is further defined in the curriculum, which states several aims of study:

The national curriculum for geography aims to ensure that all pupils:

- develop *contextual knowledge of the location of globally significant places* – both terrestrial and marine – including their defining physical and human characteristics and how these provide a geographical context for understanding the actions of processes
- *understand the processes that give rise to key physical and human geographical features of the world*, how these are interdependent and how they bring about spatial variation and change over time
- are competent in the geographical skills needed to:

  o collect, analyse and communicate with a range of data gathered through experiences of fieldwork that deepen their understanding of geographical processes
  o interpret a range of sources of geographical information, including maps, diagrams, globes, aerial photographs and Geographical Information Systems (GIS)
  o communicate geographical information in a variety of ways, including through maps, numerical and quantitative skills and writing at length.[4] [emphasis added]

The emphasised statements give an initial indication of what could contribute to the development of **assessment objectives (AOs)**. AOs are typically drawn from learning objectives and identify specific knowledge and skills that are measurable in an assessment. Some example AOs for geography are given below:

- Demonstrate knowledge of locations, places, processes, environments and different scales.
- Demonstrate geographical understanding of:

  o concepts and how they are used in relation to places, environments and processes;
  o the interrelationship between places, environments and processes.

(Continued)

- Apply knowledge and understanding to interpret, analyse and evaluate geographical information and issues and to make judgements.
- Select, adapt and use a variety of skills and techniques to investigate questions and issues and communicate findings.

The development of AOs inform the creation of tasks that specifically target them. This is decided upon once assessors have made decisions concerning the weighting of AOs across the assessment, the intended demand of the assessment, and the overall blueprint for how the assessment will be designed. The tasks, whether a set of examination questions, practical tasks or coursework, are then developed alongside the mark scheme (for practical steps to improve mark scheme design, see **Chapter 3**).

THERE ARE 'THREATS' TO VALIDITY THAT WE TRY TO REDUCE THROUGH GOOD DESIGN

Assessment practitioners have to be aware of aspects of assessment that contribute to a lesser degree of validity. A 'threat' to validity is something about the development, process or delivery of an assessment which means that the construct is not being measured precisely. There could be many reasons for this, but assessors generally categorise two main types of threat:

Construct-irrelevant variance: Factors affecting student assessment performance that are not linked to their ability in the area of interest. These may be related to the testing environment, item bias or marking reliability, for example.

Construct under-representation: Factors related to the design of the assessment which mean that the knowledge, skills and understanding we are interested in are not being covered fully.

Let us look at an example to illustrate these two ideas. Consider a teacher who is thinking of changing a classroom topic test from a paper-based assessment to an on-screen equivalent. How does this remove (or perhaps introduce) threats to validity?

The movement to on-screen testing will potentially increase the precision of the assessment, reducing construct-irrelevant variance. Data from previous versions of the test could be used, for example, to check the quality of the items and content coverage (for more on how items can be analysed for quality using data, see **Chapter 8**). The movement to on-screen may also increase the potential to use the data from the assessment to track the progression of students over time, which might align with certain purposes of the assessment, such as the diagnosis of student misconceptions.

However, there may be new factors that influence student performance on the online assessment, such as typing speed, familiarity with using computers, on-screen reading ability, and so on. These could be new threats to validity that should be carefully considered before technological innovations are implemented on a larger scale. In **Chapter 15**, we explore the future role of technology in assessment in more detail.

VALIDATION IS ABOUT COLLECTING EVIDENCE TO SUPPORT THE CLAIMS THAT YOU WANT TO MAKE

While validity is the central concept to keep in mind when thinking about your assessment design and delivery, *validation* refers to the procedures undertaken to collect 'empirical evidence' (in Messick's words) regarding the adequacy of the inferences that you want to make based on assessment outcomes. There are many reasons why a practitioner would be motivated to investigate the validity of their assessments, and some illustrative examples are provided below:

- A teacher trying to establish whether internal school mock examinations test the same things as high-stakes external examinations in the same subject.
- An employer checking whether an apprentice's assessment results are a valid reflection of their performance in the workplace.
- A regulator testing whether it is safe to allow a candidate to practise in their profession.
- A multinational assessment organisation checking whether the scores obtained in their tests reflect the abilities of students within the countries where data were collected.

The first point to make here is that validation is often conceptualised as an ongoing process, with no fixed end point. Some theorists argue that validation evidence needs to be collected constantly as the conditions around the assessment (e.g. who is taking the assessment) change.[5] Indeed, some assessment organisations have dedicated validation and research teams whose main role is to collect and interpret validation evidence in this way!

In other contexts, such as the classroom, where time is a precious commodity, this is unrealistic. Helpfully, other theorists have argued that the amount of empirical evidence required for validation is directly proportional to the size of the **claims** that you want to make.[6] Compare the following two examples of claims:

1. This qualification prepares students for their further study, including university or the workplace.
2. This assessment provides teachers with useful information regarding their students' knowledge of fractions.

Claim 1 relates to the role of the qualification (and its component assessments) in connecting students to their next stage of life. It is making a prediction about how performance in the assessments related to this qualification should map onto later performance, either at university or in the workplace. Claim 1 (as a minimum) requires evidence to support the *predictive validity* of the assessments. This necessitates the collection and analysis of longitudinal data (correlational and predictive) looking at performance between one educational stage and another.

Claim 2 relates to an assessment that is targeting a much smaller part of the overall construct of mathematical ability, as well as the use of the assessment in terms of classroom practice. This claim is connected to *consequential validity*: Do teachers receive the information they need to support their teaching of fractions? Investigating this claim may require a check (perhaps through observation or reflection by the teacher) that the assessment is helpful in making secure inferences about students' understanding of fractions.

WHAT SOURCES OF EVIDENCE CAN YOU USE FOR VALIDATION?

The educational assessment theorist and researcher Michael Kane introduced the idea that test score validation is an exercise in building theoretical and empirical rationales to support or refute assessment score interpretations – what he called an 'interpretive argument'.[7] Stuart Shaw and Vicki Crisp built on the theoretical work of Kane to develop a framework to structure validation evidence-gathering (see Table 2.2). They argued that interpretive arguments can be built by collecting evidence in relation to a series of five key validation questions.[8]

Table 2.2 Framework of questions to support the building of an interpretive argument

Inference	Warrant	Validation question
Construct representation	Tasks elicit performances that represent the intended constructs.	1. Do the tasks elicit performances that reflect the intended constructs?
Scoring	Scores/grades reflect the quality of performances on the assessment tasks.	2. Are the scores/grades dependable measures of the intended constructs?
Generalisation	Scores/grades reflect the likely performance on all possible relevant tasks.	3. Do the tasks adequately sample the constructs that are set out as important within the course content/ syllabus?
Extrapolation	Scores/grades reflect the likely wider performance in the domain (i.e. non-testing situations).	4. Are the constructs sampled representative of competence in the wider subject domain?
Decision-making	Appropriate uses of scores/grades are clear.	5. Do stakeholders know what scores/ grades mean and how they should be used?

When looking to validate an assessment, Shaw and Crisp suggest that evidence should be collected either to find evidence in support of validity or identify potential threats to validity. Identified threats to validity can then be the focus of remedial activity or development.

If, for example, we are focusing on the first and second validation questions in Shaw and Crisp's framework for a large-scale assessment, one possible source of evidence comes from the examiners conducting the marking. The most senior examiners typically produce reports where they give their views about how well students have understood the demands of the assessment, any unusual occurrences, and the quality of marking from the cohort of examiners. These reports can potentially reveal threats to validity, such as students answering items in unexpected ways. Unexpected responses from students (perhaps from a poorly worded item) would represent a threat, as this suggests that the tasks set are not representing the intended construct appropriately. For the second validation question, we might be interested in marking reliability data or more qualitative information such as mark schemes. If there is evidence here for lower-than-expected marker agreement or poorly constructed mark schemes, then these would also represent threats to overall validity (to learn more about how marking reliability is analysed in large-scale examinations, see **Chapter 6**).

REFLECTION

Think of an assessment that you have used recently.

1. What claims are made about the assessment?
2. What evidence is available for you to check the validity of the claim (or claims) made about the assessment-takers based on their scores?

Some examples of possible sources of evidence are provided below:

- course syllabus/specification;
- topic coverage grids/documentation;
- question papers;
- mark schemes/rubrics;
- marking data (e.g. mark distributions, correlations between different assessments);
- question error reports;
- teacher or student letters of complaint;
- grading reports;
- teacher reports.

INTERPRETING CLAIMS FROM ASSESSMENT OUTCOMES

Earlier in the chapter, we outlined the thinking of Sam Messick, who argued that validity is the degree to which interpretations about assessment-takers based on their performance can be substantiated. Consider the three students in the following table, who have taken a set of qualifications at age 18 with the intention of going to the same university to study psychology.

Table 2.3   Grade outcomes for a sample of 18-year-old students

	Subject 1	Subject 2	Subject 3
Student 1	Mathematics – A	Psychology – C	Biology – B
Student 2	History – B	Psychology – B	Chemistry – B
Student 3	Mathematics – B	Biology – B	Chemistry – A

The qualification grades represent an overall judgement about each student's ability in each subject. A standard claim made by assessment organisations is that the grades achieved are closely aligned with the abilities of students, and will therefore predict later performance at university. This has been explored statistically in the UK with a range of commonly taken general and vocational qualifications.[9]

Which of the three students outlined here would you think has the best chance of performing well as an undergraduate psychology student based on their qualification outcomes? One claim that could be made is that students who have previously taken a qualification in psychology will perform better than students who have not. This could be because they have acquired relevant knowledge and skills prior to entering the university programme. Evidence for this claim would be student 2 performing the best at university compared to the two other students.

Another claim may be that end-of-schooling qualifications are best thought of as a generic indication of overall student ability, and that university performance is predicted by this general ability level. Indeed, many studies that look at predictive validity or comparability of one set of qualifications to another often use the 'mean average grade achieved' as a proxy for overall student ability. For this claim to be substantiated, you may expect student 3 to perform best at university, even given the fact that they have not previously studied psychology.

A final claim may be that a specific subject *that is not psychology* may be a strong predictor of later university performance. Science, technology, engineering and mathematics (STEM) subjects have been classed as strong predictors of later university performance across a range of subjects, including psychology.[10] Many university courses in psychology have a significant emphasis on statistical analysis and biopsychology, which may provide an advantage to students that have a background in these areas. If this claim is true, then you might expect student 1 to perform best at university.

FINAL THOUGHTS

Validity has been identified as the most important concept in educational assessment. In this chapter, we have explored both how validity can be conceptualised and how validation can work in practice.

When practitioners discuss validity, reliability is often mentioned in the same breath. Reliability is a necessary, but not sufficient, condition for a good degree of validity. We explore the concept of reliability in more detail in the next chapter, where we will consider its connection to validity alongside more practical considerations, such as assessment manageability and mark scheme (or rubric) design.

KEY TAKEAWAYS

- Good assessment maintains a strong logical link between the defined construct and the assessment tasks that attempt to elicit the construct.
- Potential 'threats' to validity can be found at any stage of the assessment process. Identifying these threats is an important and useful stage of assessment design and evaluation.
- Validation is the process of collecting evidence to substantiate the claims that you want to make about assessment-takers based on their scores. There are a variety of qualitative and quantitative data sources that can be used to argue for strong or weak validity.

3

RELIABILITY

EXPLORING THE CONSISTENCY OF ASSESSMENT

IN THIS CHAPTER, YOU WILL:

- explore the relationship between assessment validity and reliability;
- learn about the factors that contribute to high or low levels of assessment reliability;
- develop methods for improving assessment reliability through effective mark scheme (rubric) design;
- gain an overview of several methods for estimating assessment reliability.

What does the word 'reliability' mean to you? In common usage, you may think of reliability as synonymous with other words such as 'trustworthy'. If you were to say that a car was 'reliable', you would be making a statement about the likelihood of it working upon command with no intermittent faults, and no need to have it fixed aside from perhaps routine maintenance. In this everyday use, 'reliable' means that something can be relied upon.

In educational assessment, the technical definition of 'reliable' is narrower and refers to the *consistency of measurement*. A fundamental question for educational assessors is the degree to which two identical assessment occasions ('occasion' being defined as the period from initial assessment design to final grading) would provide the same result. This is slightly different to the 'trustworthiness' definition of reliability used in common language. If you assessed whether a car would function or not when you turned the ignition key, a car with no engine would in fact have very high reliability, as it would consistently *not* start. In this sense, it would be reliably unreliable!

Ensuring a sufficient degree of assessment reliability is an important contributor to overall assessment validity and stakeholder confidence. However, there is a natural tension between ensuring both assessment validity and reliability. While there are steps that assessment practitioners can take to increase the consistency of measurement, there are often risks to the overall quality of the assessment in terms of it accessing the desired constructs. The tension between assessment validity, reliability and manageability is what we first explore in this chapter.

This chapter then reviews potential sources of unreliability. Unreliability in assessment emerges from the fact that assessment involves humans – we judge, we have biases, and we make errors that all can contribute to less reliable assessments. In the practical application boxes of this chapter, a framework is presented that aims to support marking reliability through effective mark scheme design. Finally, this chapter outlines some of the most prevalent statistical methods for estimating reliability.

THERE IS A NATURAL TENSION BETWEEN ASSESSMENT VALIDITY AND RELIABILITY

In **Chapter 2**, we introduced some of the key ideas around the concept of validity. We explained that validity is the primary concept to hold in mind when thinking about good-quality educational assessment. While validity takes precedence as the overall concept that informs good assessment practice, it is impossible to consider validity without also considering reliability. As Barbara Moskal and Jon Leydens state:

> Although a valid assessment is by necessity reliable, the contrary is not true. A reliable assessment is not necessarily valid.[1]

Phil Stock illustrated the idea of reliability using an analogy of weighing scales.[2] If someone was to stand on a set of weighing scales ten times over the course of a minute, they would expect the reading produced to be consistent from one occasion to the next. This expectation would hold no matter where the scales were placed in the house, the position of the feet for each measurement, or other conditions such as changes in room temperature. Of course, there is always some measurement 'error', even in circumstances that are highly controlled such as when using weighing scales. Exploring reliability is the investigation and measurement of this error.

Assessors need to be aware that measurement error exists and put good practical measures in place to make sure it does not reach unacceptable levels. The degree of unreliability of measurement that is deemed acceptable or unacceptable is at the heart of assessment design and practice. This point is illustrated by a report published in 2013 by the National Foundation for Educational Research (NFER) in the UK:

> We may choose to accept the lower levels of reliability associated with certain question types, where we believe the question type to add value over more tightly constrained questions.

However, for questions that do traditionally have lower levels of reliability, it may be possible to make improvements by, for example, refining the mark scheme or by improving marker training.[3]

In his book *Testing Times: The Uses and Abuses of Assessment*, Gordon Stobart describes this trade-off between validity, reliability and manageability as part of assessment design and delivery.[4] While the target for all assessment should be a high level of construct validity through the use of authentic assessment tasks, Stobart argued that this was in many cases unrealistic as it would result in either an unwieldy set of assessment tasks (i.e. low assessment manageability) or issues related to the reliability of the judgements made by assessors. He illustrated these tensions using the concept of the 'one-handed clock' (see Figure 3.1).

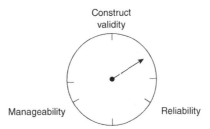

Figure 3.1   Stobart's one-handed clock

The one-handed clock represents the trade-offs that assessors need to consider. High construct validity (number 12 on the clock) may have to come at the expense of manageability and reliability. A highly reliable assessment (around number 4 on the clock) may come at the expense of manageability and overall construct validity. In practice, assessments often fall somewhere in between these extremes, and the assessment practitioners must judge the most appropriate balance in their context.

Let us consider a couple of examples. Think of a teacher who is developing an end-of-term assessment for their students. The assessment's sole purpose is to identify who understands the content covered across the term, in order to help the teacher plan for when students return from holiday. The designated purpose of the assessment means that the teacher can focus their 'hand' on the one-handed clock relatively close to construct validity. Depending on the subject discipline and area, this leaves a wide array of potential assessment tasks, including peer work, presentations, multiple-choice tests, and so on.

If the teacher is also concerned with ranking the students in order of ability, then the position of their 'hand' on the one-handed clock will move more towards reliability. This is because placing each student on a scale of ability requires that judgements are consistent enough for the teacher to rank students based on sound evidence. As we will see below, there are many sources of unreliability, some of which are related to assessor judgement.

Now let us think about an example of an assessment that is about as high-stakes as it gets: the assessment of commercial airline pilots. Due to the highly regulated, skilled and responsible nature of the job role, there is a great emphasis on authenticity of assessment in pilot training. Manual handling of the aircraft, handling skills in a wide range of situations (e.g. visual approach, landing, go-arounds, missed approaches, etc.) and crew management are all elements that are covered in a range of different scenarios. For commercial pilot qualifications, assessment comprises many hours in highly expensive and realistic simulators, assessed test flights with instructors, and – finally – observed flights with more senior colleagues (eventually with passengers on board!). This contributes to the overall length and cost of the training programme and the assessment. In this example, the emphasis is on construct validity and reliability, at the relative expense of manageability.

REFLECTION

In **Chapter 1**, we looked at some of the different purposes of assessment. Think about one or two assessments that you know well. For each of these assessments, consider:

* each purpose you have for the assessment(s);
* where you would place the assessment(s) on the one-handed clock.

1. Does the position on the clock vary depending on the purpose?
2. Does the position on the clock influence your thinking about how well your assessments meet their purposes?

THERE ARE MANY SOURCES OF UNRELIABILITY IN ASSESSMENT

We have introduced reliability as related to the consistency of measurement. It is important to understand where unreliability can creep in during the assessment process. There are multiple sources of potential unreliability, and some are outlined below.[5]

Student performance: If a student attempts an assessment several times, even if no learning takes place, the student will not get the same score each time. Their performance might be influenced by internal factors, such as their level of anxiety, general health, tiredness, and so on, or external factors, such as whether the assessment is being administered in the morning or the afternoon and the conditions of the room where the assessment is happening. If you conduct an assessment twice – once before a period of learning and once afterwards – you will expect some variation in performance from one testing occasion to the next. This may be desirable if you are looking for progress in relation to overall learning objectives or outcomes. However, you may expect a strong correlation between performance at testing point 1 and testing point 2.

Content sampling of the assessment: An important stage of assessment design is to think about the process for sampling content across the programme of study in a systematic way (see **Chapter 2**). In addition, there may be a requirement to reduce the predictability of questions. In practice, this often means that assessors sample from different parts of a curriculum from one assessment occasion to the next. If some students have particular strengths or weaknesses, this may affect their performance.

Inter-marker reliability: Despite the best efforts of assessment organisations and assessors in terms of training and monitoring, there may be instances where one assessor is more lenient or harsh compared to others, or inconsistent in their application of the assessment criteria. The movement to online marking of qualifications in the past decade means that assessment organisations can monitor examiner marking quality in much greater detail (we explore this further in **Chapter 6**). Inter-marker reliability issues can be reduced by effective training, standardisation, monitoring, and documentation that allows for similar interpretations of the marking standard.

Assessment tasks and activities: Related to content sampling and inter-marker reliability is the issue of assessment tasks. In general, the more 'unconstrained' an assessment task, the more likely that different assessors will arrive at different interpretations of the qualities of the response.[6] For instance, marking reliability for an objective multiple-choice item is much higher than that for an open-ended essay question which requires an extended response.

Differences in assessment specifications: What is considered important to learn changes over time, and this is reflected in curriculum documents and learning aims, and subsequently assessment specifications. In the UK, the first **General Certificate of Secondary Education (GCSE)** assessments were taken in 1988 and the first **A levels** were taken in 1951. There have been several changes in the syllabuses, specifications and assessment models between those dates and the present day, the most recent being between 2015 and 2017.

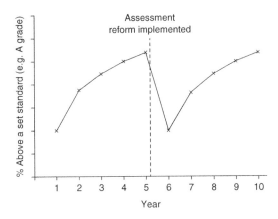

Figure 3.2   Representation of the 'Sawtooth Effect' caused by assessment reform

An outcome of qualifications reform is that teachers and students need to get used to any new course content and associated assessments. A well-known outcome of introducing new assessments for previously existing qualifications is the 'Sawtooth Effect', where performance is adversely affected in the first year following reform. This is followed by improving performance over time as students and teachers gain familiarity with the changes introduced (see Figure 3.2).[7]

Good assessment attempts to reduce the fluctuations of assessment scores or grade outcomes caused by the sources of unreliability outlined above. As Dylan Wiliam noted, the unreliability inherent within an assessment must be small in comparison with the amount of information gained about the individual.[8]

PRACTICAL BOX 3.1

TYPES OF MARK SCHEME

One reason for poor inter-marker reliability can be confusing, misleading or inappropriate mark schemes. Mark schemes (also referred to as rubrics) are a central point of reference for examiners at each stage of the marking process. Well-designed mark schemes (supported by assessor training) enable assessors to make accurate judgements of students' responses to items.

A useful categorisation of types of mark scheme was provided by Tisi and colleagues.[9] They stated that there are three main types of mark scheme:

Objective mark schemes are used when the potential range of responses to an item or task are constrained, such as a multiple-choice question or when a one-word answer needs to be provided. Objective mark schemes include only the small range of possible correct responses. They are typically applied with a high degree of accuracy.

Points-based mark schemes are used for items or tasks that range from a few words to a short paragraph. A unique element of points-based mark schemes is that the number of marks available directly matches the number of relevant points that must be made. If, for example, there is a question worth three marks, then the response will require up to three credit-worthy points. There may be more credit-worthy points possible than marks available, and these points are listed in full in the mark scheme.

Levels-based mark schemes are used when the item or task requires longer, typically more unconstrained responses from the student, such as extended writing. Because student responses can vary greatly in focus and quality, generic level descriptors are used.

(Continued)

> Levels-based mark schemes can be further divided into *holistic* and *analytic.* Holistic levels-based mark schemes require the marker to make an overall judgement of performance. Each level of performance may have several elements contained within the description, but the markers attach their own weighting to each feature.[10] *Analytic* levels-based marks schemes comprise descriptions for each of the aspects of interest at different levels (such as assessment objectives).
>
> In practical box 3.2, there are a set of principles for how you can utilise these types of mark scheme most effectively to contribute to good reliability.

HOW CAN ASSESSMENT RELIABILITY BE ESTIMATED?

Various statistical methods are used operationally and in research to measure assessment reliability. In this part of the chapter, we will outline examples of commonly used statistical approaches and how they are applied:

- test-retest reliability;
- internal consistency;
- inter-marker reliability;
- classification accuracy.

TEST-RETEST RELIABILITY

Test-retest reliability analyses the extent to which repeated assessment occasions are correlated to each other. For this method, the same assessment is administered to the same assessment-takers on two occasions after a set time. The correlation between the scores achieved on the two test administrations is then calculated. If assessment-takers perform similarly on both testing occasions, then there is a good degree of reliability.

Correlational studies of test-retest reliability show the relationship between testing occasions. They do not, however, show exact agreement of marks or grades. This is important in assessment as we are normally using the currency of assessment marks or grades in everyday contexts. If the rank order of student performance between testing occasions 1 and 2 were similar, but they all performed significantly worse on testing occasion 2, it would be hard to claim test-retest reliability.

It is also important to note that we might indeed expect a degree of improvement between testing occasions 1 and 2. The degree of improvement expected may be influenced by educationally relevant factors such as student maturity or teaching interventions. One must therefore be careful to establish a suitable protocol for assessment data collection, such as keeping only a short time period between testing occasions.

INTERNAL CONSISTENCY

Internal consistency is the degree to which items in an assessment that are claimed to cover the same construct produce similar results. For example, if you ask a student two questions related to the construct of 'reading comprehension', then you would expect a strong positive correlation between student performance on those two items.

At the assessment level, you would expect that if you had developed your entire assessment with the aim of targeting the same construct, assessment-taker performance on individual items and groups of individual items would positively correlate to one another.

This thinking underpins one method of calculating internal consistency, called the 'split-half method'. In this method, an assessment is randomly split into two halves, and the sum scores of the two halves are compared as if they were two separate administrations of the same test.[11] The correlation between the total scores of the two halves is an estimate of the internal consistency of the assessment. The split-half method is useful because it can be calculated even when an assessment is only administered once.

Cronbach's alpha (α), perhaps the best-known method for estimating internal consistency, is an extension of the split-half method. Cronbach's α is calculated by working out the correlation of all possible split halves for a particular assessment, and then calculating the average correlation. This is reported as a figure between 0 and 1. A high α indicates that the items within an assessment are highly correlated, which suggests good internal consistency.

However, it is important to note that there are several factors which will influence overall α. For example, longer assessment (in terms of the number of items) will generally result in a higher α. Furthermore, assessments with a higher proportion of objectively marked items (e.g. multiple choice) tend to have a higher α. Finally, there also tends to be a higher α if the assessment itself is doing a good job of discriminating between the higher- and lower-performing assessment-takers.

The degree to which internal consistency is important to assessment practitioners depends somewhat on the target of the assessment tasks and their intended uses. For example, if you have planned to assess two sub-constructs that are not related to one another, then internal consistency measures are of less importance compared to other reliability measures such as inter-rater reliability (see below). If you are interested in learner performance on specific items rather than across the entirety of the assessment, then internal consistency will also be less important to calculate.

INTER-RATER RELIABILITY

Inter-rater reliability refers to the degree to which marks assigned to an assessment are reproduced by different markers. Below are some easily calculated measures that can be used to determine the degree of inter-rater reliability:

Proportion agreement: This is the raw agreement of marks given by a set of examiners for an item or assessment, given as a value between 0 (no agreement in the marks given) and

1 (total agreement in the marks given). For objective items such as one-mark multiple-choice questions with only one correct answer, proportion agreement is an effective measure of inter-marker reliability. It is therefore helpful in determining the *accuracy* of marking.[12]

Proportion agreement is also useful for less constrained assessment task types, such as essays, but should be used with caution. The proportion agreement as a measure of inter-marker reliability is typically calculated using a *definitive mark*, which is a mark given for an item or assessment that is most representative of a 'true' score. A 'true' score is a theoretical concept that is defined as the individual's score on an assessment if there was no **measurement error**.[13] The 'true' score is not directly observable, but can be estimated using a range of highly complex psychometric methods.

The definitive mark for an item or assessment is commonly decided upon by one senior marker, or after panel discussions. Definitive marks are commonly used in large-scale assessments as part of the routine monitoring of marking quality (for an overview of how these data are used, see **Chapter 6**). While this is a relatively simple process for objective items, less constrained items often have a range of marks that could legitimately be argued to be the definitive mark.

Average absolute deviation (AAD) from a 'definitive' mark: One method for taking into account the possibility that markers may have different, although legitimate, views on student responses is to consider the average distance markers are from the definitive mark. Calculating the AAD is useful for getting a sense of the variation around the definitive mark, which may indicate higher or lower degrees of inter-marker reliability.

It is important, however, to contextualise these data when making a judgement as to whether marking is sufficiently reliable. For example, high-tariff questions that use levels-based mark schemes generally have a greater degree of marking variability compared to lower-tariff items that use a points-based mark scheme. In large-scale assessments, this difference is often operationalised by the introduction of a tolerance for an item or assessment. The tolerance is the degree of variation from the definitive mark that is permitted before concerns are raised about a marker's reliability. The tolerance is generally larger for items or assessments where there is a greater degree of professional judgement required during marking.

PRACTICAL BOX 3.2

PRINCIPLES OF MARK SCHEME DESIGN – THE CARFE MODEL

The difficulties in establishing high levels of reliability using levels-based mark schemes have led to a body of research investigating how mark scheme features can support the overall quality of marking. Bringing this literature together, we list five principles that practitioners can think about when developing their mark schemes – what we have called the CARFE model (see Table 3.1):

C: *Connect* the item and the mark scheme.

A: *Anticipate* the range of student responses.

R: *Reduce* marking complexity where possible.

F: *Format* the mark scheme to improve the user experience.

E: *Evaluate* the performance of the mark scheme.

Table 3.1   Mark scheme design principles: the CARFE model

Principle	Description	Practical actions
C: *Connect* the item and the mark scheme.	The specific components of an assessment item or task influence how students respond. For example, student responses may be influenced by: • expectations of the student (e.g. similar questions encountered in the past); • command words used (e.g. 'describe', 'evaluate', etc.); • paper layout (e.g. answer space); • response prompts (e.g. whether the number of desired responses has been labelled). Assessors should consider these factors when thinking about what is worthy of credit.	• Develop question and mark scheme drafts simultaneously. • Think about how questions will be interpreted by students. • Think about how many levels of response you could realistically differentiate between when judging responses. Research suggests that five is towards the top end of differentiation.[14]
A: *Anticipate* the range of student responses.	Items and mark schemes are often designed and delivered without any prior testing. This can create circumstances where students respond to questions in unanticipated ways.	• Think about what responses are 'logically derivable' from the item. • Ask a second person to answer the item. Did they answer in the anticipated way?

(Continued)

Table 3.1 (Continued)

Principle	Description	Practical actions
	Unexpected responses can usually be catered for by making final refinements to the mark scheme.	• Are there any ways that you can pretest without risking the security of the assessment? • Consider past items that you have created which are similar to the item. Did the mark scheme for the past item account for all of the responses?
R: *Reduce* marking complexity where possible.	The structure of the question and the mark scheme influence the cognitive processes underlying markers' scoring.[15,16] Assessment items that require markers to scrutinise unexpected responses are more likely to result in lower reliability compared to simpler items.	• Provide *item-specific* guidance to illustrate information included within each level of the generic marking criteria. • Refer to key points in the mark scheme during a standardisation process. • Reduce the number of marks within levels. • Define what is **not** worthy of credit.
F: *Format* the mark scheme to improve the user experience	Mark schemes are the primary point of reference for examiners, and thus need to have a high degree of usability. Research has found that small changes to the formatting of mark schemes can improve usability ratings and overall marking quality.[17]	• Think about the use of a mark scheme as a working document – either printed or on-screen. Can you make important parts of the mark scheme more visible? • Reduce the overall size of the mark scheme to one page for easy review. • Include indicative content alongside the levels of the mark scheme to which it refers. • Use bolding of key terms to maintain their salience.

Principle	Description	Practical actions
E: Evaluate the performance of the mark scheme.	Investigating item-level data can reveal potential issues worthy of further investigation (see **Chapter 8**). For example, you may find that marks are 'bunched' in the middle of the mark range or that some marks appear to be underutilised.[18] This does not necessarily mean that there is an issue with the mark scheme, but will help to plan discussions with people using the mark scheme to identify any issues.	• Consider the mark distribution data for your items. Does it appear that some marks are being over- or underutilised? • Check if the full range of marks within each level is being used. If not, this might suggest that examiners are not sure how to select a mark within levels. • Provide information in the mark scheme about how to select a mark within a level.

CLASSIFICATION ACCURACY

It is common for high-stakes assessments to go through a set of procedures that set the standard for key grade outcomes (see **Chapter 5**). Classification accuracy refers to the extent to which a group of assessment-takers would receive the same grade (or 'classification') were they to go through the same assessment experience again.

When grades are used in assessment, classification accuracy becomes important because reported grades are often the mechanism from which inferences about assessment-takers are made. Measurement error through marking inaccuracies at the *item* or *assessment* level can be somewhat tolerable to stakeholders if the final *grade* outcome is accurate (a kind of 'all's well that ends well' effect).

There are several factors that can influence classification accuracy, including the number of grades available, the width of the grade boundaries, variability in content coverage for assessments year to year, marking inconsistency, and the overall length of the assessments.

Although the specifics of the methods for determining classification accuracy are very complex and nuanced, researchers often apply the same fundamental steps.[19] First, they model all the assessment-takers' 'true' scores. Based on the estimation of the 'true' score, the 'true' grade can then be estimated, and finally compared to the observed grade outcome.

Research which estimated the classification accuracy of a set of GCSE and A-level qualifications taken between 2008 and 2009 found that for 89 per cent of the candidates across all of the qualifications analysed, students' 'true' grades either matched with their actual grade or were one grade adjacent.[20] Although this overall classification accuracy may appear low, particularly in a high-stakes environment, it is important to put the findings into context. For example, there may be legitimate reasons why assessments within qualifications have been designed with an increased risk of unreliability. This returns us to the idea of Stobart's one-handed clock and the tensions between validity, reliability and manageability.

REFLECTION

In this chapter, we have introduced different methods for estimating reliability.

- Which estimates of assessment reliability do you currently use in your practice?
- Which estimates of reliability do you think would be helpful to apply in your context?
- Which estimates of reliability are most important to you in making a strong case for assessment validity?

FINAL THOUGHTS

Reliability concerns the consistency of measurement and is fundamental to consider when looking to establish assessment validity. Assessors are trying to strike a balance between targeting a construct and securing consistency of measurement without creating assessment tasks that are unwieldy and unmanageable. Assessment manageability does not just concern the process of developing and delivering the assessment itself, but also its monitoring and validation.

The degree to which you want to explore the sources of unreliability and seek solutions depends somewhat on the initial purposes that you have for your assessment. For example, if you have set a classroom quiz with the intention of identifying specific scientific misconceptions, it is less important to check for inter-rater reliability compared to a higher-stakes end-of-year summative assessment in history.

Reliability is also a necessary factor underpinning assessment fairness, which we explore in the next chapter. Fairness is a specific validity issue that concerns the removal of extraneous factors on assessment performance. Inherent unreliability in an assessment design or procedure will contribute to unfairness. For example, it could be claimed that an assessment is unfair if the systematic variation in how examiners apply a mark scheme significantly contributes to inaccurate grade outcomes. While there is a general acceptance that there will always be some unreliability of assessment, there is a broader debate concerning how assessment can remove systematic bias and improve accessibility through innovations in task-setting, item design and on-screen assessment.

KEY TAKEAWAYS

- Reliability is necessary, but not sufficient, for assessment validity. There is a three-way tension between validity, reliability and manageability of assessment.
- There are numerous sources of unreliability that occur at different stages of assessment design, administration, processing and grading.
- Effective mark scheme design can facilitate a common understanding among assessors for how responses should be credited.
- The most appropriate statistical methods for estimating reliability depend on the purposes of the assessment.

4

FAIRNESS

IN THIS CHAPTER, YOU WILL:

- explore how fairness in assessment can be conceptualised and understood;
- investigate practical methods to review assessment questions for accessibility and bias;
- consider the connection between assessment fairness and broader educational equity.

Consider the story of two identical twin boys who began the process of learning to drive. The twins received the same amount of lessons with the same instructor, used the same car, and booked the practical test to be taken on the same day. It was generally agreed that both twins were of very similar driving ability at the point that they took the practical test.

On the day of the practical test, the older twin went first. He was asked to perform a manoeuvre where he had to reverse the car around a corner on a flat piece of road. About halfway into the manoeuvre, a white van suddenly appeared from the rear, which he did not initially see. He continued to reverse for around a second before spotting it and braking. Because of the delay in seeing the van, the examiner judged that he lacked the sufficient observational skills to be allowed to drive independently, and he was failed.

The younger twin then proceeded to take his test with a different examiner. He was also asked to perform the reversing manoeuvre. On this occasion, a large lorry came from the rear, more slowly and more visibly compared to the white van in his brother's practical test. He was therefore able to see the lorry before it became a danger, and thus took timely and appropriate action. The examiner decided that the second twin was a competent enough driver to pass the test.

We may all have assessment experiences such as this one, where seemingly random events in our assessment experience seem to determine our fate. In the case above, the two twins had a very similar degree of ability, but a combination of events led to very different assessment outcomes – and raises questions about test fairness. The older twin could complain that the van appearing at speed behind him was 'unfair', especially when he learned of a crucial difference in his brother's experience later that day. However, it could be argued that as practical driving tests are designed to sample real-life driving on public roads, *any* situation encountered in a test would be a fair assessment experience.

In recent years, fairness has become a major focus of assessment theory, both for large-scale high-stakes assessment and classroom-based assessment practice. Over the years, there have been a variety of high-profile legal cases where assessment outcomes have been challenged on fairness grounds.[1] In the first part of this chapter, we will explore what can be meant by fairness in assessment. This chapter focuses on using procedural definitions of fairness (i.e. the degree of appropriateness and comparability of assessment procedures and process).[2] The second part of this chapter focuses on how *bias* and *accessibility* issues can affect assessment fairness, as well as exploring methods for assessment review that can facilitate the identification of issues at the assessment design stage. Finally, there is a brief discussion of the role of assessment in facilitating greater educational equity.

THERE ARE INTERRELATED CONCEPTS OF ASSESSMENT FAIRNESS

It has been suggested by Tina Isaacs and colleagues that for an assessment to be deemed fair:

> the content, its context and the expectation of the assessment's performance should provide all candidates with an equal opportunity to demonstrate their ability.[3]

This view has parallels with the idea of construct-irrelevant variance that we covered in **Chapter 2**. If assessment-takers' performances are somehow impinged by an event in the testing process (e.g. a fire alarm during an examination) or a characteristic that they have which is not relevant to the construct being measured (such as their race or socio-economic status), then there may be a case to argue that the assessment was unfair.

In assessment-related discourse, debates around fairness tend to focus on potentially disadvantaged groups or subgroups of test-takers. In the UK, the Equality Act 2010 was designed to protect people from discrimination, harassment and victimisation. It defines nine protected characteristics that provide a useful framework for conceptualising particular subgroups who might be unfairly penalised in assessment (see Table 4.1).[4]

Table 4.1 Protected characteristics under the Equality Act 2010, UK

Protected characteristic	Description according to the Equality Act 2010
Age	A person belonging to a particular age or range of ages.
Disability	A person has a disability if she or he has a physical or mental impairment which has a substantial and long-term adverse effect on that person's ability to carry out normal day-to-day activities.
Gender reassignment	The process of transitioning from one gender to another.
Marriage and civil partnership	A union between a man and woman, or between a same-sex couple.
Pregnancy	Pregnancy is the condition of being pregnant or expecting a baby. Maternity refers to the period after the birth, and is linked to maternity leave in the employment context. In the non-work context, protection against maternity discrimination is for 26 weeks after giving birth, and this includes treating a woman unfavourably because she is breastfeeding.
Race	Refers to the protected characteristic of race. It refers to a group of people defined by their race, colour, and nationality (including citizenship) ethnic or national origins.
Religion or belief	Religion refers to any religion, including a lack of religion. Belief refers to any religious or philosophical belief and includes a lack of belief. Generally, a belief should affect your life choices or the way you live for it to be included in the definition.
Sex	A man or a woman.
Sexual orientation	Whether a person's sexual attraction is towards their own sex, the opposite sex or to both sexes.

These characteristics (and others, such as socio-economic status) are important to hold in mind when considering where unfairness may manifest itself in the assessment process. Isabel Nisbet and Stuart Shaw have argued that the focus on groups or subgroups of test-takers rather than individuals is in part a result of the statistical methods used to 'discover' unfairness, which rely on sufficient sample sizes to perform psychometric analyses.[5] When subgroup membership is small, it means that analysts are less confident that variation in performance is due to an unfairness inherent in the assessment.

In the 2014 edition of the *Standards for Educational and Psychological Testing*, known informally as *The Standards*, there was a new chapter dedicated to fairness, which explains four 'views', outlined in Table 4.2 below.[6]

As you read through the views of fairness outlined in Table 4.2, you might think about some examples. For instance, if there was a breach in assessment or item security which meant that some students had prior access to items before sitting an examination, that would violate view 1 of fairness on the basis that students had different opportunities to demonstrate their knowledge or skills. If there was a student who suffered from anxiety or other mental health issues related to the use of a closed-book examination, then this may violate view 4 of fairness. We will use the four views of fairness to frame the rest of this chapter. Specifically, we will look in more detail at views 2 and 3 – measurement bias and accessibility to the construct.

Table 4.2   'Views' of fairness – adapted from *The Standards*

View of fairness	Explanation
1. Treatment during testing process	This view suggests that all assessment-takers should have the same opportunity to demonstrate their abilities regarding the construct of interest.
2. Lack of measurement bias	This view suggests that assessment-takers' performance should not be influenced by their position in identifiable subgroups (e.g. gender).
3. Access to construct as measured	This view suggests that assessment situations should enable all assessment-takers in the target population to demonstrate their standing on the construct without advantage or disadvantage by individual characteristics (e.g. disability).
4. Validity of individual test score interpretations for intended uses	This view suggests that assessments should take into account individual characteristics of the assessment-taker and how they interact with the contextual features of the test situation.

REFLECTION: THE FAIRNESS OF NON-EXAMINED ASSESSMENT (NEA)

One of the 'views' of fairness introduced in Table 4.2 relates to the idea that a fair assessment both has a high degree of validity and is sensitive to the contextual features of the assessment situation. For many years, there has been a debate concerning the relative advantages and disadvantages of non-examined assessment (NEA) forming part of high-stakes qualifications.[7] NEA (sometimes referred to as internal assessment) gives teachers or students an element of control in either the task-setting or the marking of student responses (for further analysis of how NEA can function in schools, see **Chapter 7**).

One side of the argument is that fairness is improved through teachers (and to an extent students) having some control of the testing situation – fairness of treatment during the assessment process (view 1). The other side of the debate argues that this approach is unfair because it increases the risk that teacher-set tasks might not align closely to the construct or that marking reliability might be compromised – fairness as access to the construct measured (view 3).

You may have come across three main approaches to NEA in summative assessment:

- *No NEA permitted*: All assessment for a qualification is conducted through a process of paper-based examinations.
- *Controlled assessment*: NEA is conducted in the classroom under tightly regulated conditions (e.g. time limitations) and marked by a teacher. This assessment may contribute a set percentage of the overall qualification.

(Continued)

- *Coursework:* NEA is conducted over a period of time decided by the teacher. The teacher is responsible for marking student work. This assessment may contribute a set percentage of the overall qualification.

1. What issues related to fairness can you identify for each of these assessment approaches?
2. Imagine that you are considering using these assessment approaches. Which do you think is the fairest to the students that you plan to assess?

WHERE CAN BIAS CREEP INTO ASSESSMENT?

View 2 of fairness, outlined in Table 4.2, identifies measurement bias as being an important issue. Two main categories of bias are *offensiveness* and *unfair penalisation.*[8,9]

Offensiveness occurs when negative stereotypes or perceptions of certain subgroups are presented in an assessment. Offensiveness can also be a distraction for students who are taking the assessment, making them underperform relative to subgroups who are not offended. This form of bias is generally rare in standardised assessment, although it can occur in more informal assessment scenarios such as interviews or classroom assessments.

Unfair penalisation occurs when a student's test performance is distorted because the content of the assessment, although not offensive, disadvantages a subgroup of students, resulting in reduced performance. Possible subgroups can be based on the characteristics listed in Table 4.1.

EXTENSION BOX 4.1

UNINTENTIONAL BIAS IN ASSESSMENT – THE USE OF NEGATIVE MARKING

What is so difficult about the concept of bias in assessment is that it is often unintentional. Let us look at an example of True-False-Abstain (TFA) multiple-choice questions. For TFA multiple-choice items, students can either select true or false, or abstain from giving an answer. Selecting an answer that is incorrect results in a penalty – this is a form of what is known as *negative marking.*

The intention of TFA assessments is that students are encouraged to show a degree of honesty with their knowledge. This is important in contexts such as medicine, where high levels of competency have to be demonstrated in order to ensure the safe treatment of patients. However, they may also introduce other effects such as increased test anxiety.

Research has found that there tends to be a weak but systematic bias in favour of males when negative marking is used in multiple-choice tests.[10] One explanation for this effect is that males generally score higher in terms of risk-taking behaviours. This introduces the possibility of a construct-irrelevant advantage for males in TFA assessments.

Bringing us back to the broader idea of fairness, the use of TFA introduces another interesting issue: Is it fair to remove marks previously acquired on one part of a curriculum because students selected an incorrect answer on a different part of the curriculum? Recently, medical educators have attempted to move away from TFA, and instead have looked to reward certainty using a novel method called *elimination testing.*

In elimination testing, for each item students are asked to eliminate 'definitely wrong' options from each multiple-choice item. Eliminating all of the incorrect options from the possible answers is rewarded with the maximum score available, while partial knowledge can be shown and rewarded if students are unsure about which answer is correct.[11] The advantage of this approach is that students can demonstrate when they are certain of a correct answer but without the anxiety of having previously earned marks potentially removed.

DETECTING BIAS WHEN DESIGNING ITEMS – THE USE OF CHECKLISTS

Reviewing items for bias is a difficult task. One reason for bias in assessments and items is that it is difficult to detect, despite the best efforts of item writers and reviewers.

How can we, as assessment practitioners, detect bias in our assessments? One method is to bring unconscious thinking into explicit discussion by using systematic checklists. Atul Gawande, in his book *The Checklist Manifesto,*[12] argued that the use of checklists has been revolutionary in informing sound decision-making in high-stakes scenarios, such as during surgical procedures or when dealing with unexpected events when flying aircraft. Checklists have also been introduced in the process of identifying common errors in assessment design, such as formatting errors or ambiguous terminology.

Table 4.3 is a checklist for item bias that draws upon Gawande's principles, as well as the work of Hambleton and Rodgers,[13] who identified three areas of assessment item bias: content, language, and biases in item structure.

For this checklist, we need to define a broad name to account for different subgroups, so we have used Hambleton and Rodgers' term *designated subgroup of interest* (DSI). The checklist is presented as a series of questions that ask reviewers to actively confirm for each item whether they have considered each potential issue. Each checklist question response should be 'no' if the item is free of bias.

Table 4.3   Item bias detection checklist

Bias type	Checklist question
Content bias	Does the item contain content or examples that are more or less familiar or of interest to particular DSIs?
	Does the item contain material that is controversial, inflammatory or potentially offensive to particular DSIs?
	Does the item depict any stereotypes for particular DSIs in terms of characteristics or job roles, or through inappropriate images?
Language bias	Does the item contain words not related to the subject discipline or construct that would be more or less familiar to particular DSIs?
	Does the item contain unnecessary DSI-specific language, vocabulary or pronouns?
Item structure	Is there an unequal balance across the assessment in the use of names across different DSIs?

PRACTICAL BOX 4.1

BIAS IN ITEM DESIGN

Below are some question examples. Work through each one using the checklist in Table 4.3 and think about where there might be any biases.
   Try to redraft the questions to reduce the bias.

1. Write a story about a girl who goes on holiday and gets stranded on a desert island in a remote and beautiful place.

   Try to make your description of the place as vivid and interesting as possible.

2. Stefan and Dev are playing marbles.

   Stefan has 36 marbles and Dev has 45% more marbles than Stefan.

   How many marbles does Dev have?

3. Look at what the following children have for breakfast.

   Which is the most nutritious?

   Tick **one**.

   Muesli and orange juice

   Chocolate cereal and milk

   Fried eggs and toast

   Jam sandwich and cola

ONE ELEMENT OF ASSESSMENT FAIRNESS IS ACCESSIBILITY

The items or tasks contained within any one assessment are designed with the intention of sampling an element of a specific construct. One element of a valid and fair assessment is that it can isolate the targeted construct. As Vicki Crisp notes:

> Whilst part of the difficulty of an examination task will be due to the intrinsic demands of the subject content, features of the way that questions are asked (e.g. presentation, wording) can affect the actual difficulty, sometimes in unexpected or unfair ways.[14]

It has been argued that assessment design fundamentally comprises two tasks: to define the constructs to be tested, and to determine how the constructs will be assessed to provide maximum accessibility to the population of required test-takers.[15]

Accessibility as a term encompasses the related concepts of *demand* and *difficulty*.[16] Demand can be conceptualised as a judgement made on the cognitive operations that a student needs to access to answer items correctly. Alastair Pollitt and colleagues suggest that demand is a pre-test concern that utilises subject expertise to understand the requirements of the student for any one item.[17] Difficulty is a post-test analysis that can be statistically determined and which can be context-dependent. Differences in the difficulty of individual questions depend on the features of the question in terms of accessibility, in addition to the demands that the assessment developers intended. Assessments can be placed on a spectrum from 'no accessibility' to 'optimum accessibility', with placement on this continuum dependent on how effectively the items access only the target construct.

But how do we improve assessment accessibility in practice? One method is through what are known as 'access arrangements'. Access arrangements are 'pre-examination adjustments for candidates based on evidence of need and normal way of working',[18] and are specifically designed to allow learners with special educational needs or temporary injuries to access the assessment without changing its demands. For example, students might be given additional time to remove the possibility of a construct-irrelevant factor (e.g. reading or writing speed) inadvertently affecting their performance. The introduction of additional time for subsets of students therefore attempts to resolve any potential unfairness (we discuss access arrangements further in **Chapter 14**).

What is more difficult to determine is whether the amount of additional time provided is: (1) sufficient to allow the students to perform at their best; and/or (2) inadvertently giving an *advantage* to these students. It is conceivable, for example, that the additional time provided may be overestimated, which in turn gives a subset of students more time to either complete the assessment, check their work or refine their responses.

DETECTING ACCESSIBILITY ISSUES IN ITEM DESIGN – ITEM ACCESSIBILITY CHECKLIST

The checklist in Table 4.4 for identifying accessibility issues in item design draws on work from a variety of sources, including the *accessibility review matrix*,[19] *fair access by design*,[20] and research on the optimal formatting of paper-based assessments.[21] For this checklist, the answer should be 'yes' for each checklist question.

Table 4.4 Assessment accessibility review checklist

Accessibility issue	Checklist question
Item stimulus, question stem, and answer choices	Does item stimulus only contain information relevant to the process of answering the item?
	Is the vocabulary used appropriate for the target group of assessment-takers?
	Are answer choices (e.g. for multiple-choice questions) written in plain language?
Use of images	Are the visual images used necessary in order to respond to the item?
	Do the images clearly depict what they are trying to represent?
Item formatting	Has a sans-serif font been used?
	Has bolding been used to make key item instructions more salient?
	Has white space been used to facilitate understanding of elements of the item (e.g. by spacing between paragraphs)?

EXTENSION BOX 4.2

TEST ACCESSIBILITY AND ITS RELATION TO GRADE STANDARDS

In theory, improving test accessibility reduces barriers for assessment-takers to demonstrate what they know. An anticipated consequence of increased assessment accessibility is an improvement in assessment performance of the cohort.

This intended outcome, however, introduces a couple of challenges. First, how do we know whether the changes have improved accessibility and performance for the target subgroups where accessibility has been identified as an issue?

One way of exploring this question is to look for what has been called a *differential boost* in assessment performance for members of the subgroup of interest compared to others.[22] The idea behind differential boost is that when an item is modified with the intention of improving accessibility, test scores should be increased more for the subgroup of students for whom accessibility is perceived to be a greater barrier relative to other student groups. This concept is illustrated in Figure 4.1.[23] Stephanie Cawthon and colleagues argue that if there is a similar increase in performance across *all* students targeted by an assessment, then the modification can be deemed to be reducing the demand of the item, or changing the construct being measured.

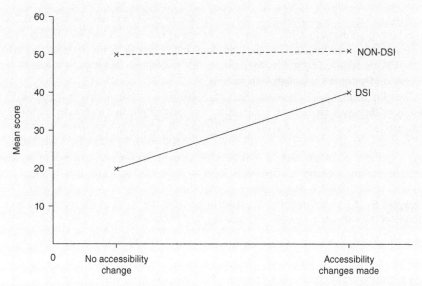

Figure 4.1   Representation of the differential boost hypothesis

The second challenge is that it is difficult to know for certain whether any improvements in student performance are due purely to improvements in accessibility or due to other factors such as the overall demand of the assessment. If the overall performance of students improves, should this be reflected in the position of the grade boundary? This question is particularly problematic for assessments developed and sat before any data about their difficulty have been collected, such as in end-of-schooling examinations. This point has been illustrated with three common arguments from stakeholders as to why changes to the accessibility of a paper should *not* influence the position of a grade boundary:

1. 'The paper is more accessible, but the amount of subject content hasn't changed.'
2. 'We've removed some of the hurdles that prevented the pupils from showing us what they could do.'
3. 'The pupils will be less 'turned off' by the paper, and so we'd expect performance to improve.'[24]

These arguments suggest that although stakeholders understand accessibility to be somewhat flexible and independent from the demands of the individual items, they may also

(Continued)

anticipate that any improvements in the accessibility of items (and whole assessments) will also benefit students in terms of overall outcomes (as demonstrated by grades). When assessment organisations declare that they have made improvements to test accessibility, it is perhaps assumed by stakeholders that grade boundaries will not change, and thus overall student grade outcomes will improve.

Tom Bramley argued, however, that accessibility is a concept which resides in the minds of the assessment community rather than something that is directly statistically observable.[25] He suggested that accessibility can be 'lumped together' with other features of items that lead to higher or lower scores on the test (such as its demand and familiarity) under the umbrella term of 'difficulty'. Changing features of an item to improve accessibility will alter the position of the item on the underlying trait, and thus the overall difficulty parameter, as calculated by statistical methods such as item facility (see **Chapter 8**). It is therefore difficult to determine what the effect of improving the accessibility of tests should be on the position of grade boundaries.

FINAL THOUGHTS

In this chapter, we have outlined the concept of assessment fairness, as well as some of the theory behind how unfairness can manifest through measurement bias and accessibility. A final question for this chapter is: How can assessment practitioners incorporate fairness in assessment, and in education more broadly?

Table 4.5 Threats to fairness – taken from *The Standards*

Threat to fairness	Explanation	Example
Test content	Test content that confounds the measurement of the target construct.	A test of reading comprehension that uses a text which favours students from a particular socio-economic status.
Test context	Aspects of the test and testing environment that might affect the performance of an assessment-taker differently to other assessment-takers.	A test item requiring unnecessarily high levels of linguistic understanding to access the demands of the item.
Test response	Where items in the test elicit unexpected responses or can be solved in ways that are unintended.	Fine motor skills required for extended writing.
	Where tests propose challenges in terms of response not related to the construct.	
Opportunity to learn	Exposure to instruction and knowledge that affords students the opportunity to learn the content and skills required for the test.	Inequities in school resources lead to a reduction in opportunity for students.

The Standards is again useful in this regard. In Table 4.5, there are four 'threats' to fairness that are connected to the different stages of assessment design, construction and response. The threats listed relate to the assessment instrument itself and the immediate testing environment, as well as broader 'macro'-level factors.

The final threat to fairness listed here – opportunity to learn – raises an important issue about the role of assessment in broader society and the mechanisms for how equity can be achieved. Equity is not just the opportunity to learn inside a classroom, but also students' opportunities to enjoy similar facilities, resources, materials and cultural capitals prior to the assessment event.[26,27] While assessment practitioners are duty-bound and motivated to refine their assessments to remove the possibility of unfairness in the assessment process, there may be limitations in how far assessment can go to ensure educational equity.

KEY TAKEAWAYS

- Fairness in assessment is the consideration of assessment-takers' needs to allow them to demonstrate their ability in the construct targeted by the assessment.
- Bias or issues with accessibility of assessment can be difficult to detect, but systematic and careful analysis of assessment design and processes can support overall fairness of assessment.
- While fairness in the design, development, processing and grading of assessments is important in the argument for validity, there is also a broader question of how fairness prior to assessment events can be established.

5

STANDARDS

ARE THINGS AS THEY 'USED TO BE'?

IN THIS CHAPTER, YOU WILL:

- learn how standards can be conceptualised;
- learn how to adapt the demands of individual assessment questions;
- explore the potential for 'reference' tests to be used to support standards maintenance.

If you have been lucky enough to attend university but 'unlucky' enough to be the second (or later) generation in your family to go, you have probably had a discussion with an older relative about how 'easy' it is to achieve a high university grade compared to when they went to university. This claim is typically based on the observation that an increasing proportion of students are achieving the higher degree classifications. In Figure 5.1, you can see the percentage of students in UK universities who received the top degree classification, known informally in the UK as a *first*, from 1995 to 2017.[1]

What can explain this observed increase in firsts over time? Your relative may suggest that there has been some fall in *standards* at university. For example, they might argue that the content taught, the assessments, or the processes for judging performance mean that students need less 'ability' to achieve the higher classifications. In their view, if a student were to go to university in 1995, they would be less likely (all other things being equal) to achieve the higher classifications compared to if the same student went to university in 2017. This perception of a reduction in standards has been called **grade inflation**. To use the high jump as a sporting analogy, the bar to a *first* has been lowered.

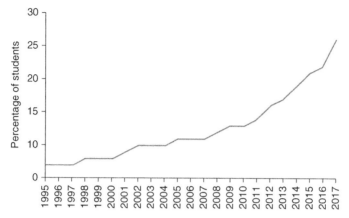

Figure 5.1   Proportion of students awarded a first for their undergraduate degree (1995–2017)

If you asked a lecturer, teaching fellow or student to explain the data in Figure 5.1, they may point to advances in the educational experience before or during university. Their argument may be that positive changes in teaching quality in schools and universities have contributed to an increase in the 'ability' of a typical student entering university, as demonstrated by grade profiles (see Figure 5.2)* or the amount that students can learn during their course (e.g. due to quick access to online journals). In their view, although the high jump bar has remained broadly the same, more students are able to clear it successfully.

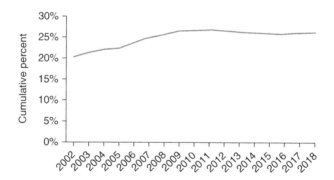

Figure 5.2   Percentage A grades at A level – all subjects[2]

Perceptions of educational standards are a key motivator for reform, including changes to large-scale and high-stakes assessments. While the term 'standards' is used in many ways in

---

* The proportion of A-level students achieving an A or A* has been static from 2010 to 2017. This is due to the 'comparable outcomes' approach to standard-setting that was introduced in the UK from 2010 to curb grade infla-tion (to read more about this approach, see **Chapter 6**).

education and assessment, it is perhaps too broad a term to be immediately useful. Two people discussing 'standards' may really be talking about different things. There is also a great degree of variability in how 'standards' as a term is understood within single nations and internationally. In this chapter, we outline some of the different notions of standards and how they relate to one another.

We will also explore some of the practicalities of setting and maintaining standards over time at both the question and qualification level. Lena Gray and Jo-Anne Baird, in their introduction to a special issue of the journal *Educational Assessment* on standards, highlighted three systemic-level factors that influence how standard-setting is conducted:

- policy and political structures;
- assessment paradigms;
- governance structures.[3]

These influences, and their historical contexts, have afforded a great deal of variability in methods of standard-setting and maintenance, with each process utilising a range of judgemental and statistical data to varying degrees. In this chapter, we define key concepts that inform standard-setting from theoretical and operational perspectives so that you have a sound understanding of the different factors which influence how students are differentiated from one another.

The final part of the chapter explores an approach that has been recently adopted in the UK to create an objective measure of whether educational standards have changed over time: the National Reference Test (NRT). The intention behind the NRT is to inform standard-setting and maintenance for large-scale national assessments, by giving an indication of how one cohort of students compares to previous cohorts in terms of their performance standards.

THERE ARE DIFFERENT TYPES OF STANDARDS

As mentioned in the introduction, when people talk about *standards* in educational assessment, they are often discussing slightly different things. Below are three types of standards that are commonly referred to in educational discourse: assessment standards, performance standards and content standards. Let us look at each one in turn.

ASSESSMENT STANDARDS – WHAT IS TESTED

Assessment standards refer to the *demands* of a particular assessment, as well as whether students have learned what they are supposed to have learned.[4] It has been argued that there is no statistical method for measuring assessment demands, and thus we often rely on the experience and judgement of professionals (see **Chapter 4**).[5] However, there may be some features of assessments that indicate different levels of demand, including the length of the assessment, the amount of 'work' to be done in the assessment time frame, and the amount and difficulty of reading.

It is difficult to find a large-scale assessment that *has not* been subject to ongoing discussions about its demands. Debates hinge around whether assessments need to be more practical or more theoretical, the choice of topics, and so on. These debates are further complicated by the fact that different kinds of assessment are demanding in different ways. If you are learning a foreign language, being confident speaking and communicating is not the same as knowing a lot about how the grammar of the language works. While both are useful to ensure a rich understanding of language, they draw on very different skills.

The question that assessment developers need to answer is: Which knowledge and skills are most important to target when designing an assessment? It is possible to manipulate the intended demand of an assessment (see practical box 5.1), but there needs to be careful consideration of what you may expect assessment-takers to produce in response to the set tasks.

PRACTICAL BOX 5.1

CHANGING THE DEMANDS OF ASSESSMENT ITEMS

Qualitative methods to conceptualise assessment demands have been developed in the past 20 years. One method called *CRAS* uses four dimensions (complexity, resources, abstractness, strategy) to help structure comparisons across items:[6,7]

- *Complexity*: This is the number of components, operations or ideas that need to be linked together in order to answer an item. This can be likened to the levels in Bloom's taxonomy, with simple operations requiring knowledge recall, and more complex tasks involving evaluation, creation or knowledge utilisation.
- *Resources*: This is related to the extent to which assessment-takers are given the information needed in order to answer the question, or whether they have to generate it themselves. For example, in mathematics, you may change the demand of an item by providing or removing a useful formula.
- *Abstractness*: This is the degree to which the assessment-taker has to deal with concrete or abstract ideas.
- *Strategy*: The degree to which the most appropriate strategy for answering the question is provided to the assessment-taker, or whether it has to be devised independently.

Using this framework, it is possible to consider how questions can be adapted to either increase or decrease their demands. For example, taking the last dimension – strategy – it is possible to reduce the demand of an item by making the approach to answering a question more explicit. Compare the two examples of an English literature question on Shakespeare's *Twelfth Night*.

(Continued)

1. What are your impressions of Malvolio?

2. What are your impressions of Malvolio?

In your answer, you should consider:

- his position in Olivia's household;
- his puritanical ways;
- what he does and the ways others treat him;
- the language that he uses.

Example 1 requires unconstrained extended prose. The assessment-taker must make several decisions about how to formulate their response, perhaps by searching their recollections of Malvolio's key actions during the play. In example 2, the assessment-taker is given guidance as to what is relevant to their response. While there remains an expectation that responses will be in extended prose, the overall demand of the item is reduced as the assessment-taker does not need to anticipate the expectations of the examiner.

It is important to note here that changes to an item such as in the examples above will also require changes to the mark scheme (for principles of mark scheme design, see **Chapter 3**). In this case, providing the students with the strategy for responding to the item will: (a) reduce the likely range of responses observed; and (b) make it necessary to provide guidance to assessors about how to score student responses that deviate from the suggested response strategy.

PERFORMANCE STANDARDS – WHAT IS ACHIEVED

Performance standards concern how well something has been done, as represented by an overall score or grade. For general qualifications, such as those at the end of schooling, there are several performance standards, occasionally referred to as *grade standards*. For assessments that have the purpose of defining whether a student should be given a licence to practise, there is often a single performance standard.

Michael Kane, whom we met in **Chapter 2**, makes the distinction between the *performance standard*, which he defines as a conceptual notion of the minimal level of competence, and the *passing score*, which is the operational representation of the performance standard. Gregory Cizek argued that although this distinction is important to understand from a theoretical perspective, in practice the two terms are often used synonymously.[8] When setting the performance standard, a group of experienced and knowledgeable practitioners are in essence determining which score on the assessment scale (an operationalisation of 'ability' in the construct targeted) best represents a minimally competent performer.

A further point is that performance standards are often contextually bound. If you ask a university student and a 14-year-old student the same question on the topic of history (e.g. 'Discuss the causes of the Great War'), we would anticipate different levels of performance. For each age, assessors need to decide what level of performance is deserving of each grade or mark.

CONTENT STANDARDS – WHAT IS TAUGHT AND LEARNED

Content standards (sometimes referred to as educational standards) are defined as the outcomes, curricular objectives or specific instructional goals that form the domain from which an assessment is constructed. Assessment performance is designed to be interpreted in terms of the content standards that the assessment-taker, given their score, is expected to have attained. Content standards are therefore represented by the assessment.

Out of the types of standard we have outlined above, the one that takes precedence often relates to the purposes to which we want to put the assessment results (for an outline of possible assessment purposes, see **Chapter 1**). Let us look at the example of assessments that take place at the end of schooling. If the purpose is for selection (e.g. for entry to university), then the proportion of students being awarded each grade (the performance standard) is very important to you. If the purpose is not for selection, but rather to represent a basic level of attainment in a range of subject disciplines or skills, then your interest will be in who has achieved that basic level of attainment (the assessment standard).

To use another example, when assessing with the aim of determining workplace or vocational competence, then the requirements placed upon students are a priority. This will mean that content standards, as well as their relation to assessment standards, are particularly important to consider. In **Chapter 15**, we discuss how authentic assessment connects to ideas of content standards.

HOW CAN WE SET STANDARDS?

Perhaps the best-known definition of standard-setting was provided by Cizek. He defined standard-setting as:

> the proper following of a prescribed, rational system of rules or procedures resulting in the assignment of a number to differentiate between two or more states or degrees of performance.[9]

This definition gives the impression that the process of standard-setting is largely a technical issue – the enactment of mutually agreed procedures for differentiating one level of performance from another. However, as Cizek later observed, standard-setting is where aspects of good measurement collide with social, emotional, political and economic forces.[10] Returning to the UK universities example mentioned in the introduction, lecturers assign marks that have a direct correspondence to an (often fixed) mark at different levels of degree classification.

An advantage of this approach is that students immediately understand how their mark on any assignment contributes to their overall final degree classification or grade. The use of fixed boundaries in this way has been argued to be beneficial in terms of transparency.[11] Interestingly, the standard-setting and -maintaining processes in universities also have historical weight, either at department, faculty or university levels. This makes it difficult to alter the position of the classification boundaries, even when other external forces (e.g. increased consumerism from increased tuition fees, pressures from the **National Student Survey**, etc.) are creating the conditions for more lenient marking, for instance.[12]

In day-to-day practice, standard-setting is the *operationalisation* and enactment of rules and procedures to differentiate between levels of performance.[13] The aim of setting **cut scores** is to ensure that from test to test, assessment-takers of equal ability are rewarded to the same extent by accounting for differences such as the difficulty of the assessment or the cohort of students taking the assessment.

Many different standard-setting methods exist, each with their own positive and negative aspects. They can be divided into two main categories: cohort-referenced and criterion-referenced.

Cohort-referenced methods calculate cut scores by controlling the number of candidates receiving each grade. For example, the worst-performing 50 per cent of candidates taking the assessment in any one assessment event will fail. Cohort-referenced methods are useful in situations where there is competition for places, such as when selecting a top-performing proportion of a cohort. This is because it becomes relatively straightforward to manage the flow of students from one educational stage to another. The main issue from a validity perspective is that cohort-referenced approaches do not refer directly to the construct being assessed, but rather the performance of candidates relative to others. This may mean that two students of the same ability in different years may receive different grade and educational outcomes, depending on who happened to be in their cohort.

Cohort-referencing is often referred to as *norm-referencing*, although there is in fact a subtle difference. In norm-referencing, a previously tested population (the norm group) is used to initially develop an assessment with known properties, such as standardised scores. The norm group comprises a carefully selected and stratified sample. The second group then takes the assessment, and their performance is compared to the norm group.

Criterion-referenced methods determine the cut score by referring to a defined standard, as represented by a curriculum or other documentation. This approach means that theoretically, all assessment-takers could achieve their desired grade outcomes, depending on whether or not they meet the minimum defined standard for the assessment. For criterion-referenced methods, standard-setting procedures attempt to determine what is acceptable and unacceptable performance related to specific criteria. This approach to standards is underpinned by the idea that subject discipline or teaching experts can create both assessment tasks and criteria which can be compared to student performance outcomes. Of course, this is not straightforward, and in many cases a weaker form of criterion-referenced methods is applied where judgements on grading decisions attempt to take into account variability in the difficulty of assessments.[14]

MAINTAINING STANDARDS

How can we be sure that an A grade from 2000 means the same as one from 2015? For this, we have to look at methods for maintaining standards over time.

A first consideration for maintaining standards comes at the assessment design stage. The creation of a detailed assessment specification, or 'blueprint', can be utilised over the life of a qualification or specific assessment to ensure a comparable content coverage, assessment demands and test construction year-to-year.

The setting of grade boundaries can be considered a standards maintenance procedure because grade boundaries are meant to represent the same ability over time. Different sources of evidence are used to determine where the grade boundary for any one qualification should sit, including information concerning the general ability of the cohort, evidence about the difficulty of the assessments, and finally evidence of the standard of work produced.[15]

Occasionally, there may be changes to an assessment specification, such as after a period of qualifications reform. When this occurs, the 'Sawtooth Effect', which we illustrated in **Chapter 3**, becomes more likely as teachers and students adjust to the new qualification and assessment methods. We are likely to see in the first few years that students underperform compared to students of a similar ability in the years before reform. If major changes are made to the syllabus or the test specification, these must be taken into account when trying to make the results of the new assessment comparable to the old one.

EXTENSION BOX 5.1

THE USE OF REFERENCE TESTS TO MAINTAIN STANDARDS

One of the main challenges of the debate on changing standards over time is that it is difficult to establish a fixed, objective point of comparison from cohort to cohort. One method to track genuine improvement in educational standards has been the use of reference testing.

Reference testing has been used to support standards maintenance across a period of qualifications reform. Hong Kong used reference testing between 2010 and 2012 when they introduced new assessments in core school subjects.[16] A similar approach has recently been adopted in the UK with the introduction of the National Reference Test (NRT). The NRT was commissioned by Ofqual and developed by the National Foundation for Educational Research (NFER). The NRT aims to collect evidence on changes in performance standards, specific to the same content that is tested in the end-of-schooling assessments in English language and maths in England.

(Continued)

Just under 20,000 students take the assessment in each subject per year, and they are carefully sampled across around 330 schools. The assessments are taken in February and March before the main examination period, which begins in May.[17] Alongside the administration of the NRT, Ofqual conducts additional analysis to consider the prior attainment profile of the sample of students who take the test, as well as conducting a survey to explore student motivation to participate in the NRT and the end-of-schooling examinations.

There are some crucial features of the NRT that make it possible to inform standard-setting and standards maintenance. First, the NRT comprises some of the same questions each year, which makes it possible to compare across cohorts using **item response theory (IRT)** analyses. Second, the assessment is delivered securely, which means that the potential for item exposure is reduced. Third, the NRT is not used as part of any school accountability metrics, which reduces any temptation to 'game' the assessment.

The NFER first developed precise estimates of the percentages of students each year achieving the equivalent level to three key GCSE grades in 2017: grades 4, 5 and 7 (grade 1 being the lowest passing grade, and grade 9 the highest). These estimates were then used as a baseline to compare with future cohorts.[18]

In 2019, Ofqual used the outcomes from the NRT to inform the awarding of grades for the first time. The broad approach was described by Chris Wetton and colleagues as follows:

1. Data outcomes from the NRT for the years 2017, 2018 and 2019 were analysed concurrently so that ability distributions could be produced for the 2017, 2018 and 2019 samples on the same scale.
2. The distributions from 2018 and 2019 were mapped onto the 2017 baseline to produce estimates of the percentage of students at the same level of ability in those years. This was done for each of the three key grade boundaries. The percentage of students at each grade threshold or above in 2018 and 2019 could then be established.[19]

The outcomes comparing the 2019 cohort to the 2017 baseline are summarised in Table 5.1.[20]

Table 5.1 Outcomes from the NRT for English language and mathematics

Subject	Year	Grade 4 and above	Grade 7 and above
English language	2017	69.9 (±1.9)	16.8 (±1.3)
	2019	65.8 (±1.7)	16.0 (±1.4)
Mathematics	2017	70.7 (±1.4)	19.9 (±1.3)
	2019	73.1 (±1.3)	22.7 (±1.3)

Table 5.1 indicates a difference in the pattern of change between subjects. For English language, there was a reduction in the estimated percentage of students who would

achieve grades 4 and 7. Ofqual interpreted this change in the context of the motivation survey, where they found some evidence that students in 2019 were less motivated compared to 2017. In contrast, they found an increase in estimates at grades 4 and 7 for mathematics. Ofqual interpreted this finding as being indicative of the 'Sawtooth Effect'. In both cases, Ofqual concluded that there was insufficient evidence to change the GCSE grade standard for either subject.

While the NRT is currently being used as a mechanism to ensure the maintenance of grade standards, it has been suggested that over time there may be a movement to use the results to inform educational policy.[21] As discussed in **Chapter 1**, however, any movement to use the NRT to gauge educational standards over time or to inform accountability metrics would introduce problematic pressures on the assessment in terms of its security and the threat of malpractice.

FINAL THOUGHTS

At the beginning of this chapter, we identified three common perspectives for how the term 'standards' can be defined. The varied definitions of standards, as well as the conceptual and technical challenges to tracking changes in these types of standards over time, leaves the door open for *claims* about standards, rather than research evidence, to inform educational policy.

In large-scale assessment, views on standards are often used to forward the argument for reforms.[22] Assessment organisations have to respond to the challenge by justifying each stage of assessment development, design and delivery. Although we tend to consider standard-setting and -maintaining when deciding final grades, there is also a requirement for every previous step of assessment design (from curriculum, to question paper design, to scoring) to embody the correct content standard. Standards are therefore created, maintained and adjusted within a community of practice comprising key actors both within and outside of assessment organisations.

For standards – and subsequently public trust – to be maintained, there is a requirement for assessment organisations to explain to stakeholders how the assessment principles that we have explored in this book are embedded into their practice. In Part B we aim to meet this requirement by offering insights into the key actions, actors and procedures that underpin valid assessment design in assessment organisations and schools.

KEY TAKEAWAYS

- There are different conceptualisations of standards. Discourse around standards is influenced by the concepts and assumptions held by individuals, institutions and the public.

(Continued)

- Frameworks such as CRAS can inform the adjustment of item demands. This can support the editing of questions for different learner types or educational stages.
- Standard-setting is defined as the following of rational rules and procedures to differentiate between levels of performance. In practice, there are technical, operational and political influences on standard-setting procedures.
- There are various sources of evidence to support the maintenance of standards over time. In recent years, the UK has introduced the NRT to offer a direct comparison of cohorts in order to inform grading decisions.

PART B

ASSESSMENT PRINCIPLES IN ACTION

6

LIFE IN AN ASSESSMENT ORGANISATION

IN THIS CHAPTER, YOU WILL:

- learn about the different stages of examination paper design;
- reflect upon a model that represents the item-writing process;
- learn how quality of marking can be monitored.

At different stages of life, whether during our schooling or in the world of work, we have all participated in assessments that have been developed by an assessment organisation. Assessment organisations (sometimes referred to as examination boards or awarding organisations) can be private enterprises, not-for-profits, charities or government institutions, and develop assessments and qualifications across a range of sectors and age groups.

We see the names of assessment organisations at key points on our learning journey. You may have memories of seemingly random letters or institution names on examination papers that appeared to change from subject to subject and year to year. Learners' experiences and interactions with assessment organisations have a role to play in how they develop their beliefs and attitudes about assessment in general. While assessment-takers and other stakeholders are primarily concerned about the final 'product' of, say, an examination paper or a final certificate, an important way to build trust within an education system is to be transparent by showing how assessment organisations function, as well as the processes they have in place to ensure assessment quality.

The focus of this chapter will be on three phases of assessment design and delivery that contribute significantly to the discourse concerning public trust in qualifications. The first phase is the *writing* of an examination paper and associated items. When we refer to an 'item' in this chapter, we mean the question or task, the marking criteria, and any other associated materials, including images or inserts. Item quality contributes to public trust in assessment systems, and any errors that make it onto the final version of the question paper can draw significant media interest. The specific processes for developing examination papers vary, but in this chapter we highlight some common stages, activities and team member roles.

The second phase of assessment design that we will explore in this chapter is the *monitoring* of examiners as they mark examination papers. As discussed in **Part A**, an element of assessment validity is ensuring that judgements of student work are informed by sound marking criteria and are not influenced by unjustifiable variability among examiners. We therefore provide an overview of common metrics that can be used to infer examiner marking quality.

The third phase of assessment design that we will explore in this chapter is the *process for finalising grade outcomes*. As discussed in **Chapter 5**, there are many different methods for setting and maintaining standards. In this chapter, we will focus on a case study of how high-stakes general qualifications in England and Wales are graded, known as the 'comparable outcomes' method.

CREATING AN EXAMINATION PAPER

When assessment is delivered on a large scale, such as for high-stakes examinations, it is imperative for assessment organisations to have an efficient, secure and high-quality set of procedures to manage the development of individual examination papers and items. Individual assessment organisations have different processes in place that are the culmination of many years of incremental improvement and refinement.

What is described in this section is not directly linked to any one question paper production process. Instead, we aim to give you an overall sense of the key activities undertaken and the main actors involved in the process.

ITEM/EXAMINATION PAPER DRAFTING

The entire process of developing an examination paper is typically overseen by at least one senior manager in the assessment organisation. Senior managers are responsible for the whole of the examination production process, monitoring marking quality and the awarding of grades. In this sense, they represent a 'common thread' throughout the lifespan of the assessment, and thus have a deep understanding of any issues that have occurred at each stage of the process. Senior managers are also responsible for the development of a 'blueprint' for each assessment, sometimes referred to as the 'assessment specification'. Assessment specifications detail key information about each item and how they relate to the rest of the assessment. They outline the weighting of assessment objectives, content areas to be covered, the marks available for each item, and the intended demand.

The early drafting of items is informed by the assessment specification. *Test authors* or *setters* (hereby setters), who are subject experts and often experienced examiners, are given the task of creating an initial draft version of the items that form an examination paper. Recent work by Martin Johnson and colleagues has identified five interconnected stages in the item-writing process (see Figure 6.1) that setters work through in creating a first full draft of the items that comprise a full examination paper.[1,2]

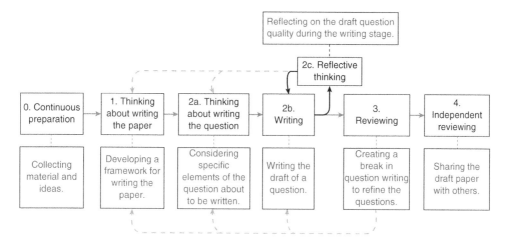

Figure 6.1   A model of item writing

0. *Continuous preparation:* Setters reported that they are often in a set of 'readiness' for item-writing. They collate interesting figures and resources during the year that have the potential to be utilised during the main item-writing process.
1. *Thinking about writing the paper:* This is the stage where setters consider the overall framework for developing and drafting the items that form the overall assessment. This stage is informed by a series of existing documents, including:

    • the overall assessment 'blueprint' set by the senior manager;
    • sample assessment materials from previous versions of the examination paper and mark schemes;
    • the specification for the qualification, including information such as the assessment objectives.

    Further activities in this stage include the identification and consideration of potential stimulus materials, such as images, diagrams or texts, potentially drawing upon research conducted in stage 0. Johnson and colleagues found that setters go through a process of making the task manageable, by either ruling in or ruling out options for the later drafting stages

2. *Writing the question*: This stage comprises three substages:

    2a. *Thinking about writing the question*: This is the first time that the setter turns their attention to individual items. The decisions made in stage 1 inform the focus of individual items, along with potential stimuli that could be used.

    2b. *Writing*: This is the first attempt at creating items and the associated mark scheme. Setters often work using a reverse logic: they consider the answers to the items before thinking about the question itself or any stimulus materials associated with it.

    2c. *Reflective thinking*: This stage provides an opportunity for further refinement of the versions of the items developed in stage 2b. Setters will consider a variety of different 'angles' in reflecting on the quality of their first written drafts. They may consider the coverage of the assessment objectives across the examination paper, elements of question quality, such as phrasing and the accessibility of items, and aspects related to the anticipated experience for the assessment-takers.

3. *Reviewing*: While stage 2c involves an element of ad hoc review as to the quality of the items comprising the assessment, the reviewing stage is a more formalised process of quality control. Typically, the setter creates metaphorical distance between themselves and the items so that they can review them more objectively. This distance may be created by returning to review items after a set period of time.

    It is at this stage that setters also begin formatting and typesetting. Setters aim to make the items look as close to the proposed final version as possible, as this provides a more authentic reviewing process.

4. *Independent reviewing*: After initial drafting, a paper is then submitted for review and refined over a series of (typically remote) interactions. In the examination paper production process, this is usually considered as its own discrete stage.

INITIAL ITEM/EXAMINATION PAPER REVIEW

The *test constructor* or *reviser* (hereby reviser) is responsible for working with the setter to take the draft version of the items and examination paper to a point where it is ready for formal typesetting and quality control checking procedures. This is part of stage 4 of Johnson and colleagues' model. For security reasons, the reviser provides feedback either in written form using software managed by the assessment organisation or by telephone. Setters and revisers are also instructed to maintain detailed logs of communications. This stage of the examination paper production process is typically conducted over several weeks, and is an important stage for identifying questions that have errors, inconsistencies or issues with accessibility.

TYPESETTING

Once a full version of the examination paper and associated mark schemes have been agreed, it is then sent for typesetting. This stage is monitored by a member of administrative staff in the assessment organisation and the senior manager. The purpose of typesetting is to create a version of the examination paper that resembles the 'feel' of the final version as closely as possible.

FURTHER QUALITY CONTROL CHECKS

After typesetting, the examination paper is then subjected to a further series of quality control checks. These checks vary across assessment organisations, but there are several common approaches that are traditionally used:

Candidate proxy: This is when an experienced examiner sits the assessment as if they are a student. The candidate proxy works through the examination paper without any access to the mark scheme. The aim of this check is to ensure that all of the items in the examination paper can be completed in the time available and are answerable. In cases where there is some optionality in the examination paper, the candidate proxy is tasked with working through each optional item, as well as commenting on their similarity in terms of demand.

Scrutineer: The scrutineer has access to the entirety of the assessment materials, including the examination paper and the mark scheme. Scrutineers are given specific instructions for how to check the paper. For example, one assessment organisation asks scrutineers to actively identify the component parts of each item, such as the command words, and elements of supporting resources that are required to answer each item.[3] The theory behind this active identification of elements of the items and mark schemes is that it makes checking a more conscious process, thus increasing the likelihood for potential errors to be noticed. This process may be conducted several times, after each iteration of the examination paper has been created and typeset.

Subject expert check: The role of the subject expert check is to provide an additional inspection of the examination paper before final approval. This check may resemble the methods used by either the candidate proxy or the scrutineer. The subject expert is not related to any previous stages of the examination paper production process.

Proofreader: Provides a standard proofread of the entire examination paper.

For each checking method, any errors or proposed changes are noted in the audit log for consideration by the senior manager and senior examiners.

COMMITTEE MEETINGS

Committee meetings are a common part of the examination paper production process, although the exact timing of these meetings varies across assessment organisations. Committee meetings are chaired by senior managers in the assessment organisation and aim to offer an additional level of scrutiny and justification for the decisions specific to the examination paper. The committee meetings are attended by the senior examiners who have overall responsibility for the quality of individual examination papers. If the committee meeting is held in order to provide final approval for an examination paper, or a set of papers, then there is occasionally one final check prior to dispatch for printing.

SIGN-OFF AND DISPATCH FOR PRINTING

At this stage, the examination paper is modified as required to make it accessible for the full range of students who are planning on sitting the examination. **Chapter 14** explains the range of options available to assessment organisations to improve accessibility.

The overall process from initial item or paper authoring to final sign-off can take up to 18 months. In many cases, two different versions of each examination paper are created, with one paper acting as a reserve in case the first paper cannot be used. The reserve paper may be called upon if an error has been detected after the sign-off stage or if there is a security issue, such as a paper being seen by teachers or candidates before testing day.

Importantly, any changes to versions of items or the examination paper are kept in an audit log. This maintains an ongoing record of interaction between assessment writers, senior members of the assessment production team, and managers within the assessment organisation. Assessment organisations use the audit log as part of a post-production review, with the aim of identifying any threats to effective paper production.

REFLECTION

We have outlined in the sections above the overall process for the development of assessment papers and individual items. Consider any instances where you have written summative assessments (e.g. end-of-year exams for your students) and think about the questions below.

- Does the item-writing model explained by Johnson and Rushton (see Figure 6.1) resemble your own assessment writing practice?
- What checks and review processes have you put in place to ensure the quality of the assessments that you have written?
- Do you think that any of the strategies for checking examination paper quality could be replicated at a smaller scale, such as in a school setting?
- Does your understanding of the examination paper development process change how much you trust large-scale assessment?

MARKING AND GRADING OF ASSESSMENTS AND QUALIFICATIONS

Each time an assessment series is run, assessment organisations use data generated from examiners to monitor marking quality. The following statistics from one such assessment organisation show the scale of the operation. These statistics relate to the 'summer' examination series between May and July 2015.[4] In this series there, were:

- 567 examination papers produced;
- 14,500 examiners who marked at least one examination paper;
- 3 million examination papers marked in total.

In this particular assessment organisation, the majority of the examination papers (99 per cent) were marked online using web-based marking software. To make online marking possible, over 52 million pages of individual student scripts were electronically scanned and stored, which were then downloaded by individual examiners.

As examiners mark, their marking data are captured, which allows the assessment organisation to monitor marking quality. This section provides an overview of the processes in place to recruit, train and monitor marking quality during a 'live' marking series.

MARKING TEAM STRUCTURE

Figure 6.2 is a simple representation of the structure of a marking team for one examination paper.

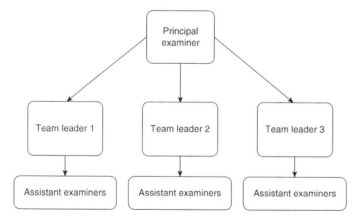

Figure 6.2   The structure of a marking team

The *principal examiner* is the head of the marking team, and there may be several principal examiners for any one qualification. The role of the principal examiner during a live marking session is to provide effective guidance and training for members of their team during standardisation, utilise available data to monitor marking quality, and provide a line of communication between the teams of examiners and the assessment organisation. Principal examiners are often highly experienced assessors who have gained promotion within their marking team over time.

Team leaders are responsible for the monitoring and support of a small team of assistant examiners. The number of team leaders required for an examination paper depends on the number of candidates taking the assessment. Team leaders typically have several years of experience as examiners. Like the principal examiner, team leaders analyse the data outputs from routine marker monitoring reports supplied by the assessment organisation.

Assistant examiners are primarily responsible for the accurate marking of examination papers. Before they are approved to mark genuine examination papers, they are first trained by a team leader or principal examiner to use the online marking software and apply the mark scheme accurately. Training may involve marking a set of examination papers that have been marked previously by the senior examination team with accompanying feedback. Once assistant examiners are marking sufficiently closely to the standard set by the senior examiners, then they are approved for marking.

CHECKING MARKING QUALITY

The principal examiner and the senior manager from the assessment organisation are responsible for any final decisions regarding whether team leaders or assistant examiners are marking to the desired standard. The change from paper-based to online marking in the past decade means that it is now possible to analyse marking data in almost real time. Team leaders, principal examiners and senior managers are now able to gather intelligence as to any trends in marking outcomes which suggest that they need to investigate individual examiners. There are several data that establish an overall view of how well examiners are marking.

In Table 6.1, you can see an example of the types of data that may be used by an assessment organisation to monitor marking quality. In this example, there are six assistant examiners who are responsible for marking an examination paper worth 50 marks and comprising questions that range between one and six marks.

Interrogating these data for each individual examiner, both in isolation and relative to each other, is a key part in understanding: (a) whether the examiners have a shared understanding of how to apply the mark scheme; and (b) whether there are any examiners who may have deviated from this understanding.

Table 6.1 Sample data for a small marking panel

Name	Number of papers marked	Mean mark	Difference from all markers' mean mark (25.15)	Number of seed scripts marked	Mean absolute total difference from seed
H. Ford	28	23.85	−1.30	12	0.5
A. Rai	81	25.17	0.02	19	1.21
J. Nicholson	145	25.72	0.57	18	0.94
S. Germanotta	160	21.14	−4.01	8	3.90
T. Hanks	120	24.96	−0.19	17	1.35
W. Goldberg	51	24.14	−1.01	13	1.38

Table 6.1 shows that the overall mean mark for all of the papers is 25.15, just over 50 per cent of the marks available for the paper. The column labelled 'Difference from all markers' mean mark' indicates the distance between each examiner's own mean mark given and the overall mean mark. This statistic gives an initial indication of potential leniency or severity of marking. It is important to consider these data alongside the number of scripts marked. If examiners have not marked a sufficient number of papers, it is difficult to be certain whether examiners may have simply marked an atypical sample of papers up to that point. The performance of examiners also are compared to what are known as 'seed scripts'. Seed scripts are examination papers that have been marked previously by a panel of senior examiners, and are randomly placed into the sets of papers that examiners download and mark. The marks attributed to the seed scripts by the senior examiners are a representation of the 'true' score for the examination paper. A significant deviation from the seed script marks indicates that an examiner might not be marking to the desired standard. The column labelled 'Mean absolute total distance from seed' indicates the average distance that an examiner deviated from the seed mark for the seed scripts that they have marked. The larger the number, the more likely that an examiner is marking poorly.

REFLECTION

Before reading on, take a moment to look at the data in Table 6.1. What numbers in the table stand out to you or look unusual?

Are there any examiners in the panel that you would be concerned about?

One thing that you might have observed reading Table 6.1 is that different examiners have marked different numbers of examination papers, with H. Ford marking only 18 per cent of the scripts marked by S. Germanotta. This is not an uncommon occurrence in teams of examiners as different examiners have different work schedules and time to commit to marking examination papers. For examiners who have not marked enough scripts, we need to be cautious when inferring about their marking quality.

You may also have observed that the mean mark for each examiner ranges between 21.14 for S. Germanotta and 25.72 for J. Nicholson. The mean mark for all of the examiners across all of the marking panels is calculated at 25.15. From these data, it is possible to gather some understanding for whether some examiners are potentially marking too harshly or too leniently compared to others. It appears that A. Rai's mean mark is well aligned with the overall mean, J. Nicholson is perhaps marking slightly generously, and S. Germanotta is marking harshly. H. Ford and W. Goldberg appear to be marking harshly; but because they have not marked that many scripts, it is perhaps too early to draw any firm conclusions.

The seed data offer some more useful insights about marking quality. Looking at the mean mark data, it appears that J. Nicholson could be marking too leniently and S. Germanotta too harshly. However, J. Nicholson has marked 18 seed scripts with an absolute mean deviation of 0.94 marks, which compares favourably with S. Germanotta's mean absolute deviation of 3.90.

There is potentially a case building that S. Germanotta might have deviated from the established marking standard set by the more senior examiners. In practice, a team leader, principal examiner or senior manager would conduct an investigation of S. Germanotta's marking, with the intention of establishing whether the data produced here are indeed indicative of poor marking quality. This may involve the interrogation of some of the examination papers that she has marked and/or checking the data to determine whether she is marking consistently harshly (as suggested by the data) or erratically. Once investigations are complete, S. Germanotta would either be allowed to continue marking as normal or be given further training, or in some cases may be asked to stop marking.

THE AWARDING OF GRADES FOR HIGH-STAKES QUALIFICATIONS IN ENGLAND AND WALES

In **Chapter 5**, we explored how assessment organisations have different processes in place for setting and maintaining the standards of their assessments and qualifications. The specific processes that assessment organisations use are determined by a range of factors, such as the regulatory framework they work within, the type of assessment or qualification, the stability of the cohort entered for the qualification, and the amount of data that are available.

In this section, we will explore the process of standard-setting and -maintaining in the context of a large assessment organisation based in England. The overall process was developed by Ofqual, the qualifications regulator for England and Wales. Below, we outline the procedure for the awarding of grades for the GCSE qualification.

THE AWARDING COMMITTEE MEETING

An important stage of the grading procedure is the awarding committee meeting. The task of the awarding committee is to recommend a grade boundary for each of the 'key grades', which for GCSEs are grades 7, 4 and 1. The awarding committee comprises a set of experienced assessment specialists who are responsible for the design and marking quality of the assessments that comprise the overall qualification. The exact composition of the awarding committee varies, but it typically has the following:

- A representative from the assessment organisation to chair the committee meeting and record discussions. They are responsible for the final grading decisions and for maintaining standards. In many cases, this is a senior manager with overall responsibility for the standards of the qualification.
- The principal examiners, who are responsible for the development of question papers and the management of teams of examiners.
- Other senior examiners such as team leaders.

The committee uses a combination of expert judgement and statistical information to inform their initial grade boundary decisions. Committee members first familiarise themselves with archive scripts that were on the boundary marks for the key grades in the previous year. They also refer to **grade descriptors**, which denote the qualities of candidates at each of the key grades. The judgements of committee members are then collated and a discussion takes place about the location of the mark boundary for each grade. The aim of using expert judgement in this way is to support the maintenance of content and performance standards (see **Chapter 5**).[5]

This decision process is supported by a range of statistical information. One source of data is mark distribution information, such as means and standard deviations. These can be useful as an initial indicator of where a change in a grade boundary may be required. A second source of data relates to prior attainment of candidates for the qualification. These data are used as part of what is known as the *comparable outcomes approach*.

THE COMPARABLE OUTCOMES APPROACH

The comparable outcomes approach was introduced as part of standard-setting and -maintaining for qualifications in England and Wales from 2011. The comparable outcomes approach aims to ensure that two successive cohorts with the same profile of prior attainment will receive broadly the same distribution of grades.

For GCSE, the comparable outcomes approach uses statistical predictions that model the relationship between prior attainment (as determined by the cohort's performance on a previous large-scale assessment taken when students were 11 years old – called the Key Stage 2 SATs) and later GCSE outcomes, using data from a previous cohort. This model is then applied to the current cohort of students. The idea is that if the current cohort have demonstrated in their prior attainment that they are of a higher or lower overall ability, then this can be accounted for when calculating grade outcomes at GCSE. If the prior attainment of the students in the current year and the reference year are similar, then the grade outcomes would also be expected to be similar.

For GCSE awarding, not all of the candidates from the cohort are included in the predicted grade outcomes. Calculations are based only on:

- candidates who are in Year 11 (age 15–16) at the time of taking the GCSE;
- candidates in maintained non-selective schools (pupils in selective or independent schools are not used within calculations);
- candidates with matching prior attainment data from Key Stage 2 SATs in English and mathematics.[6]

The prior attainment data provide a prediction of grade distribution at the qualification level that can then be used to guide final grade boundary decisions. It is expected that the predictions provided by prior attainment data match as closely as possible within set tolerances. The greater the number of candidates entered for a qualification, the smaller the permitted tolerances.

It is possible for assessment organisations to make grade boundary decisions outside of the predicted outcomes. This may be because of a disagreement between the judgements from members of the awarding committee and the grade boundaries required to fit the comparable outcomes prediction. In such cases, a further detailed review of evidence would take place and the assessment organisation would inform Ofqual of an 'out of tolerance' award. This award is subject to further checks from Ofqual to ensure that the grade boundaries can be justified.

WHY WAS THE COMPARABLE OUTCOMES METHOD INTRODUCED?

The comparable outcomes approach was introduced in response to concerns related to fairness and standards. It was observed (as you can see in Figure 5.2 in **Chapter 5**) that there was a gradual increase in the proportion of students achieving the top grades in large-scale qualifications in England and Wales. This led to accusations of grade inflation at both GCSE and A level.

What is interesting to contemplate here is that if the focus of assessment organisations was only on performance standards, rather than grade outcomes, then over time you might indeed expect to observe an increase in the proportion of students gaining the higher grades compared to previous years. This would perhaps be explained by improvements in teaching to the curriculum over time, for example. This might be seen as 'fair' in the sense that students are demonstrating more of their ability in the construct that is the focus of the assessment. However, it was argued that this would be unfair to students who had taken the same qualification in previous years, particularly if qualifications are used to distinguish students across cohorts, such as when applying for jobs.

Related to the point above, the comparable outcomes approach was introduced to defend against the possibility of the 'Sawtooth Effect' – unfairness to students who are taking a newly reformed qualification (see **Chapter 3**). Mike Cresswell of Ofqual noted that there is, on balance, an ethical imperative not to disadvantage students on the basis of deficits or advantages that are unique to a cohort of candidates.[7]

FINAL THOUGHTS

The assessment industry is growing, with an increasing number of organisations making grand claims about the quality and precision of their assessments and qualifications. Assessment organisations depend on establishing and maintaining the confidence and trust of students, educators, employers and broader society. As Dylan Wiliam noted, qualifications and assessment results are like bank notes, in the sense that 'their value [depends] on the status that is accorded to them within a social system'.[8]

This chapter has contributed to building trust in the assessment system by lifting the lid on the key processes and actors that underpin the development of large-scale and high-stakes assessments. The chapter has also shown that every practice, process and decision related to assessment is conducted by highly motivated and experienced assessment specialists who are closely monitored and supported by assessment organisations, as well as through regulatory frameworks.

The approach to comparable outcomes established in the early 2010s by Ofqual gets to the heart of tensions underpinning the maintenance of standards over time. Public awareness and understanding of these tensions are important in improving engagement with – and subsequently trust in – assessment systems. This is particularly true in periods of systemic flux, where new solutions to age-old problems are being proposed.

KEY TAKEAWAYS

- There are several interrelated stages involved in the process of writing high-quality examination items and assessments.
- Assessment organisations use different sources of qualitative and quantitative data to check marking quality.
- Grading decisions for high-stakes GCSE assessments in England and Wales involve combining expertise of an awarding committee and statistical predictions based on the cohort of students taking the qualifications.
- Assessment organisations rely on a large cohort of examiners of various levels of expertise who are regularly trained and continually monitored in their roles.

7

STANDARDISATION, MODERATION AND COMPARATIVE JUDGEMENT IN SCHOOLS

IN THIS CHAPTER, YOU WILL:

- learn about the factors that influence the consistency of judgements of non-examined assessment;
- develop principles for optimising the moderation and standardisation of assessment judgements;
- explore the debate around the use of comparative judgement in schools from a variety of perspectives.

Good assessment relies on a strong alignment between the defined knowledge, skills and/or understanding that you are looking to target, the tasks that you use to elicit evidence, and the soundness of judgements about how well the evidence produced maps onto set criteria. Although many people think of 'examinations' when they think of assessment, there are infinite other methods of collecting evidence, many of which are more suitable than examinations for one reason or another.

This chapter explores the challenges of using alternative approaches to examinations for school-based assessment. A key difference between examinations set by external assessment organisations and school-based assessment is that teachers have a degree of control over task-setting and/or marking.[1] This degree of control means that it is imperative to establish processes which espouse confidence in the reliability and consistency among assessors within and between schools, as well as maintaining standards.[2] While the focus of this chapter is on school-based assessment judgements, much of what is covered here can be generalised to any assessment context where the principles of assessment are being applied.

The first part of this chapter looks at the challenges of ensuring that assessor judgements of non-examined assessment (NEA) – also known as internal assessment – are sufficiently consistent to ensure fair outcomes for students. This is followed by an analysis of a relatively new method of marking NEA in recent years known as 'comparative judgement'. In the past decade, comparative judgement has emerged as a potential alternative to traditional marking approaches and is currently being applied in a range of educational contexts. By the end of this chapter, we hope that you have gained an understanding of some of the issues and debates around the use of comparative judgement from psychological, practical and technical perspectives.

CONCEPTUALISING TEACHER-BASED JUDGEMENTS

Chapter 3 explored how a variety of factors can influence reliability in assessor judgements. These interrelated factors on teacher-based assessment have been summarised in a recent framework, shown in Figure 7.1,[3] which built upon a previous evidence-based model of marking task demand.[4] The framework proposes that marking task demand and teacher (marker) expertise are the two overall groupings of factors that influence marking agreement. Where a marking task has higher demand (i.e. it is more difficult for the marker to carry out) or teachers have lower levels of expertise, there is likely to be a lower level of agreement (i.e. more variation between assessment judgements).

Compared to external, typically examination-based assessments, NEA has several additional factors that may influence marking reliability (the elements in dark grey):

* task control;
* feedback from moderation;
* standardisation approaches in schools;
* relationship with students;
* knowledge of student performance outside of assessment.

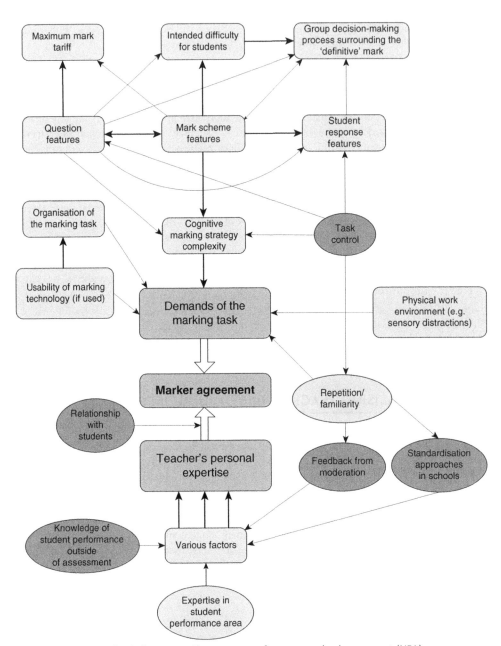

Figure 7.1   Factors that influence marking agreement for non-examined assessment (NEA)

These factors either have an influence on the demands of the marking task or on the personal expertise of the teacher (the elements in mid-grey in Figure 7.1).

As mentioned above, NEA gives teachers a degree of control over the assessment task, which may result in a greater degree of familiarity, both in terms of how to set up the task and the marking criteria used. This might support higher levels of marking agreement due to an overall reduction in the cognitive demands of marking. Because of this familiarity, marking expertise can be supported by iterative rounds of internal or external moderation feedback or standardisation.

However, NEA has the potentially confounding issue of there being an ongoing relationship between the assessor (e.g. a teacher) and the assessed (e.g. a student). In external assessment, the examiner knows little or nothing about the candidate whose work they are assessing. While pre-existing knowledge of the student may help teachers to interpret submitted evidence, it can add to the challenge of weighting assessment evidence separately from the student's performance elsewhere. This might be amplified where the mark scheme allows a degree of interpretation.

THE PROCESS OF MODERATION

Due to the inherent demands of the marking task underpinning NEA, a key factor in ensuring sufficient assessment validity is establishing and maintaining the standards on which assessment evidence is judged, as well as reaching a common understanding of any marking criteria. An approach to this quality control is that of moderation. Social moderation (sometimes known as 'consensus moderation') involves the use of learning outcomes or assessment objectives to compare the marking of assessors in different settings.[5]

Moderation is a process 'that connects the richness and authenticity of school-based assessment to increased dependability and comparability of the assessment results'.[6] It has been suggested that there are three main purposes of moderation.

- *Equity*: Achieving consistency by ensuring that assessment tasks allow all students to demonstrate intended learning outcomes, giving assessors the opportunity to develop a shared understanding of standards, as well as ensuring that standards are being applied consistently.
- *Justification*: Affording defensibility of assessment outcomes to stakeholders.
- *Community-building*: Emphasising the value of collaboration in establishing and reviewing standards, as well as developing competency in assessment design and practice.[7]

Social moderation is intended ultimately to facilitate consistency in assessor judgements, which is an important element of assessment validity. The assessment researcher Royce Sadler argued that without the opportunity to collaborate and moderate with other assessors, there will be an endemic risk to marking consistency. He suggested that the process of social moderation is beneficial because it transfers the process of marking NEA from a private process to something that is collegially held.[8]

SCHOOL-BASED MODERATION

School-based moderation of NEA aims to enable teachers to clarify and align their inter-pretations of the standards, as well as reaching an agreement about the level of achievement that each student has met.[9] Moderation may be used for informal activities (e.g. a discussion with another teacher about a student's work) or as part of a formal external process (e.g. an assessment organisation quality-assuring teacher judgements).[10] In more formal settings, such as when teacher-marked NEA is forming a component of a qualification, there is a requirement for marks to be internally moderated before submis-sion to the assessment organisation. The assessment organisation itself may then conduct their own moderation procedure.

In practice, social moderation in schools comprises a set of meetings where teachers dis-cuss examples of evidence produced by students. The focus of the meetings is to develop a shared understanding of the 'standards' related to a range of tasks. Either before or during the meetings, the assessment team will consider individual pieces of work submitted by students. The teachers consider the same submissions, so comparisons can be made of where teachers placed the work on the marking scale.

A critical component of social moderation is the review of the discrepancies between assessor judgements on the same submissions.[11] Through discussion and clarification, asses-sors gradually come to a 'consensus' on the marks or grades they would award for individual submissions. In some cases, an outcome of social moderation processes is that assessors may return to their own judgements and adjust them to bring them into line with the marking standard reached in the moderation meeting.[12]

PRACTICAL BOX 7.1

PRINCIPLES FOR EFFECTIVE MODERATION

A common conceptualisation of social moderation is that it comprises a single meet-ing (or a set of meetings) that occur(s) towards the end of an educational stage. Moderation is best considered, however, as an ongoing dialogue among teacher asses-sors as part of their developing understanding of standards. In this practical box, we provide some principles for how to frame social moderation activities to ensure a productive approach.

Maintain reference to the standard: The most effective moderation processes are when teachers can reference key documentation throughout the process. Reference to the standards may be provided in the form of performance or grading descriptors, marking criteria for an assessment task, or materials provided as part of other statu-tory arrangements such as exemplar work. It is important that these materials are readily available for those participating in social moderation, as otherwise there is a higher risk of standards 'drift' within or between meetings. Consistent referral back to standards descriptions facilitates the process of tacit knowledge being made more explicit, which is important for reaching a shared level of understanding.

Structure discussions and feedback in a non-personal way. Moderation processes should focus on the assessment evidence rather than the 'performance' of individuals who have either produced the assessment submission or have initially marked it. Where possible, moderation discussions should be considered as an opportunity to maintain a community of practice, rather than a means to establish who is a 'good' or 'bad' assessor. A focus on the latter can have a detrimental effect on the quality of moderation meetings as teachers aim to protect their status as practitioners, which can reduce the openness of the discussions. To prevent this, it is useful to clarify at the beginning of moderation that the aim is to come to a shared understanding of standards, rather than to 'root out' people who have deviated from the standard.

Avoid issues of group dynamics: As social moderation involves groups of practitioners, it is open to issues of group dynamics, such as power relations, assumed authority, and minority and majority influence.[13] Social moderation in schools ideally involves teachers who feel confident enough to support and challenge each other, as well as sharing an understanding that – at times – individuals may need to change their opinions.[14] If one teacher has a good 'feel' for the standards, or is in a position of authority to state as such, then social moderation meetings can become a more top-down dictation rather than a dialogic discussion where understanding is co-constructed. This is avoided by setting 'ground rules' so that all opinions can be heard.

View moderation as part of ongoing professional development. Related to the point above is that the most effective moderation processes are visualised as professional learning opportunities for teachers, where assessment understanding and 'literacy' can be developed.[15] Allan Luke and colleagues suggested that teachers who engage in moderation are more likely to:

- assess student performance more consistently;
- build common knowledge about curriculum expectations and levels of achievement;
- identify strengths and areas for growth based on evidence of student learning.[16]

The final point from Luke and colleagues was supported by a recent study that focused on how social moderation improved New Zealand primary school teachers' understanding of assessment for learning concepts.[17] In the study, it was found that participation in social moderation afforded the creation of a strong community of practice, facilitated the development of writing effective assessment criteria, and improved the quality of debate around developing learning outcome statements.[18]

ANOTHER WAY? COMPARATIVE JUDGEMENT FOR SCHOOL-BASED ASSESSMENT

So far in this chapter, we have looked at the factors that influence the reliability and standardisation of marking judgements in the context of school-based assessment. In regular marking, an assessor uses a set of criteria (typically a mark scheme or rubric) to make an *absolute* judgement about the evidence produced by a student. This absolute judgement is represented by the mark given. A series of these judgements results in measurements on a perceived scale of quality.[19] Assessor training, moderation, standardisation, and the features of the mark scheme are all designed to inform and improve the placement of individual students on the scale of quality. However, a known disadvantage of making judgements in this way is that individual assessors are open to biases, unreliability, and in some cases even malpractice.[20]

As discussed above and illustrated in Figure 7.1, ensuring reliable and consistent judgements becomes increasingly difficult the more 'unconstrained' a student's response to a task may be. For example, by their very nature, multiple-choice items constrain the range of responses of a student to either no response, an incorrect response, or a correct response. In comparison, a piece of creative work, such as an artist's portfolio, is unconstrained. This naturally results in a greater potential for individual assessors to arrive at different judgements about the same work.

Comparative judgement (CJ) has been identified as a potential alternative to traditional marking. In CJ, instead of assessors making a series of *absolute* judgements on submitted work, they are asked to make a series of *relative* judgements. For each judging 'event', assessors are presented with two examples of student work (labelled 'objects') and asked to select which is the better of the two. This is a holistic judgement about the overall quality of the work presented. To inform this judgement, assessors can be provided with specific criteria that lists the qualities which assessors should be considering.

The object in the pair judged the 'winner' most frequently is considered to have 'more' of the target attribute. The difference between objects' numbers of wins is assumed to be related to how far apart the objects were perceived to be in terms of the attribute.[21] When all of the paired comparisons (i.e. the comparisons from each pairing combination and all judges) are considered together, a complex statistical model is used to create an interval scale for the targeted attribute, and each object is located on the scale.[22] This scale 'represents the outcomes of the assessors' cumulative comparative judgments of the quality of the psychometric latent trait being measured'.[23] From this scale, inferences can then be made about student performance.

In the past 25 years, CJ methods have been applied in comparability studies that looked to compare standards across examination boards.[24] Recently, there has been increasing interest in using CJ in situations where conventional absolute methods of marking are deemed insufficiently reliable or time-consuming, such as for the assessment of extended writing.

WHAT ARE THE ARGUMENTS FOR AND AGAINST COMPARATIVE JUDGEMENT?

Proponents of comparative judgement claim that it has several advantages over traditional marking. These come from several perspectives, of which we will explore three here:

Psychological: It has been argued that comparative judgement is more closely aligned with how humans make judgements in the natural world. This view has been greatly influenced by the work of Donald Laming. In his book *Human Judgment*, Laming argued that 'there is no absolute judgment. All judgments are comparisons with one thing or another'.[25] Laming argued that judgemental processes are in essence ordinal; and thus while it is cognitively straightforward to judge what is better or worse, it is more difficult to decide *to what extent* one thing is better than the other. He also suggested that humans are better at comparing concrete objects with each other, rather than concrete objects with abstract concepts (such as when a student response to a task is compared to a standard represented in a mark scheme). Taken together, this suggests a psychological advantage for CJ.

Furthermore, research has suggested that traditional marking can require complex thought processes, particularly when students have responded to assessment tasks in unexpected ways.[26] Quality of marking in traditional assessment is somewhat influenced by any leniency, severity or inconsistency of assessors, whereas CJ avoids this by removing the requirement to assign a mark or grade.

Practical: In CJ, each object is successively paired with every other object and judged. For each pair presented, assessors are asked to judge which of the two objects in the pair is stronger in the targeted attribute. The evidence is currently mixed as to whether CJ approaches to judging work is more time-efficient than traditional marking methods. For example, one study from Ofqual found that although comparative judgement was more efficient than traditional marking methods that utilise **double marking**, it was less efficient than single marking.[27] While it appears more efficient to make an individual comparative judgement compared to marking an individual's work using a mark scheme, research has shown that the increase in the amount of judges required to reach good reliability levels negates much of the time saved.[28] However, this must also be considered within the context of the time and resources it takes to train and monitor judges or assessors. It might be the case that any additional costs related to CJ can potentially be offset by increases in reliability.

Furthermore, recent technological advancements have made it possible to reduce the number of judgements required to make a measurement scale.[29] For *adaptive* comparative judgement (ACJ), the pair of objects that is presented to assessors is based in part on the outcomes of previous judgements. The idea behind this is to better target the presented pairings, such as by avoiding pairings where the result of the comparison would offer little in terms of its contribution to forming the measurement scale. For instance, if an object has won most of its comparisons, it would be increasingly unlikely to be paired with an object that has lost the majority of its comparisons.[30]

Technical: The main technical 'selling point' of CJ is that the practical steps adopted to make comparative judgements, as well as the statistical analysis that underpins the development of the interval scale, result in assessment outcomes that are easily interpreted and more reliable compared to traditional methods of assessment. Research studies comparing the reliability of traditional marking and CJ generally report an advantage for CJ.[31] ACJ methods have reported reliabilities as high as 0.97,[32] although there has been recent research which has argued that reliabilities from ACJ methods are potentially inflated (see extension box 7.1).

EXTENSION BOX 7.1

THE RELIABILITY OF COMPARATIVE JUDGEMENT

ACJ methods attempt to reduce the number of judgements required to reach a desired degree of reliability. While the reliability of ACJ in fewer judgements has been listed as one of the advantages of the method, there is currently an ongoing debate as to whether the reported reliabilities from ACJ methods are inflated. A simulation study showed that ACJ exercises can inflate what is known as the Scale Separation Reliability (SSR) coefficient, which is the measure of reliability used in the research studies.[33] The study found that with adaptive methods. it would be possible to obtain a reasonably high SSR coefficient (around 0.7) even with random data, which should report an SSR of zero. Tom Bramley and Sylvia Vitello explain the reason for the inflation as follows:

> adaptivity essentially 'capitalises on chance' because all objects start out with unknown measures, and the information used to make decisions about pairings is, in the early stages, based on just a few dichotomous data points. This information is itself not reliable enough to base pairing decisions upon, and once the objects' estimated measures become spread out the adaptive algorithm is not likely to pair objects that appear to be very different, and thus the potentially disconfirming evidence for the hypothesis that they are indeed a long way apart is never collected.[34]

As part of their research study, Bramley and Vitello compared two standard CJ methods with an ACJ method and found that there was a potential 'inflation rate' of SSR between 0.27 and 0.12. With this finding, they suggest that researchers or practitioners using ACJ methods should have to prove that SSR is not inflated when using their specific adaptive algorithm.

COMPARATIVE JUDGEMENT IN THE CLASSROOM – ENGLISH WRITING

Comparative judgement offers design options that might be preferable to traditional marking procedures in certain contexts. Potential future applications include the use of comparative judgement for the maintenance of standards in high-stakes qualifications.[35] One context where comparative judgement methods may be useful are in circumstances where students are producing extended pieces of writing, portfolios or other performative responses. We will explore this idea in more detail using the example of assessing writing in English at primary school.

Writing is a key competency for young children to master, but it can be difficult to assess reliably because of the requirement for students to demonstrate complex concepts such as creativity, persuasion, tone, and sense of audience. Chris Wheadon and his team at No More Marking have used CJ as part of the Assessing Primary Writing project to explore its potential to be used at scale to inform progression.[36] The project is a study including 55,000 students ranging from Year 1 to Year 6 (age 5–11). The students were asked to produce a piece of extended writing no more than two or three sides of A4, depending on their year grouping. Teachers within schools that were participating in the study were then asked to complete a comparative judging activity where they made a series of judgements within a set marking period.

From the thousands of CJ decisions and the underpinning statistical analysis, a scaled 'quality' score for each script was calculated and all presented on one scale. The scale used was between a score of 300 and 600 (see Figure 7.2).

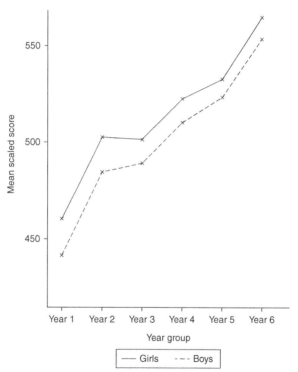

Figure 7.2 Scaled scores for Year 1 to Year 6 (non-pupil premium only) – adapted from Wheadon and colleagues

The scale in Figure 7.2 represents an increasing 'ability' in English writing. Wheadon and colleagues suggest that the overall findings show a reassuring progression between school years in writing ability. They noted that periods where progress appears to be 'flat', such as between Year 2 and Year 3, might be due to variability in the time intervals when data were collected.

A question here is: If teachers are making multiple comparative judgements, what criteria are they basing their decisions on? One of the perceived disadvantages of CJ methods for placing students on a measurement scale is that it is not always apparent what criteria have been used to judge one object as better than another. As part of the same project, teachers were observed as they worked in pairs making a series of comparative judgements.[37] Three pairs of teachers from four schools (12 pairs in total) were asked to judge a set of Year 2 (age 6–7) and Year 6 (age 10–11) scripts. Their discussions and interactions with the CJ software were captured and used to perform a qualitative analysis.

From the observations of the teachers, four main criteria were observed:

- *The mechanics of writing* – technical accuracy relating to sentence structure, paragraphing and punctuation.
- *Searching beyond the mechanics of writing* – aspects of writing related to the narrative, or the success in writing for effect.
- *Nebulous constructs* – such as 'rhythm', 'playfulness' and 'meeting the purpose'.
- *Relation to national standards* – discussions that link student work with criteria included in the national standards at different ages.

What is interesting about the criteria given above is that they were constructed organically among the teachers without initial direct reference to a mark scheme or rubric. Teachers' focus on the 'nebulous' constructs indicates elements of student responses that are difficult to capture in traditional mark scheme criteria, and may explain some of the challenges in marking extended writing reliably.

REFLECTION

You can try the overall process of comparative judgement with a few examples of work from your own context. Find several examples of student responses to a task that you set. This could be an essay, another extended writing task, or a portfolio of work.

Try putting two examples side by side and decide which is the better example. Once you have decided which is the better example, select two others and go through the same process. Over several judgement 'events', see if you can come up with a rank order of examples that you are happy with. If you have a colleague available, give the examples of work to them and ask them to go through the same process.

Once you have both got your rank orders, discuss how and why you arrived at your decisions. Did you use the same or different criteria?

You might find that you came up with different rank orders or that you had different reasons underpinning your decisions. You can use these differences to help each other understand your own personal criteria for making your judgements, as well as helping you to reach a common understanding.

FINAL THOUGHTS

Whenever schools or teachers are empowered to design or deliver assessments with a summative purpose, teachers and senior leaders are tasked with ensuring a comparability of standards across their schools. Moderation is an essential tool in ensuring a desired degree of rigour and trust in assessment or qualification outcomes. Importantly, the success of standardisation or moderation is dependent on establishing an open dialogue among practitioners.

Moderation is necessary in NEA because of the challenge in ensuring that assessors are considering student work in consistent ways. Well-known difficulties of establishing and maintaining reliability when using absolute judgements have led to a recent groundswell of interest in methods that claim to make improvements, such as comparative judgement. As we have explored in this chapter, in the context of English writing, comparative judgement has the potential to enable teachers and other practitioners to visualise progress using data that can be presented on one measurement scale. As Daisy Christodoulou argues, understanding progress is very much the holy grail of assessment in education.[38] We are not just interested in how individual students are performing relative to previous assessment events; we also want some idea of the value that schools add.

To make sound inferences and justifiable claims related to student progress or a school's capacity to improve learning trajectories, educators look to utilise data from a range of different sources. In the next chapter, we look at some principles for how assessment data can be processed, managed and interpreted to ensure strong learning outcomes.

KEY TAKEAWAYS

- The reliability of NEA teacher-based judgements is underpinned by factors that determine the expertise of the marker or the overall demand of the marking task.
- Effective social moderation relies on setting optimal group dynamics among assessors that facilitate a genuine community of practice.
- Arguments for and against the use of comparative judgement can come from psychological, practical and technical perspectives.

8

USING ASSESSMENT DATA

IN THIS CHAPTER, YOU WILL:

- consider three important foci when using assessment data to make educational decisions;
- evaluate some of the issues around the measurement and tracking of student progress;
- learn how assessment data literacy contributes to enhanced learning outcomes.

This chapter explores how we use assessment data. Schools and other educational institutions now have access to more data than ever before, but it can often be overwhelming to turn data into useful information on which educational decisions can be based. We will look at these challenges and offer some principles for thinking about assessment data, as well as examining their uses and limitations.

In their simplest definition, data comprise a set of values, such as numbers or text, that can then be used to derive information. Data have been collected and analysed throughout human history, and they increasingly play a key role in our society. Concepts of 'data-driven' teaching, learning and instruction have become increasingly ubiquitous in discussions around how learning outcomes can be improved. Furthermore, school performance tables, data-driven exam predictions, international education evaluations, and student surveys are all common features of the landscape. For example, in the UK, the use of assessment data to inform decisions related to the curriculum, learning and instruction has been encouraged in recent years by the withdrawal of **national curriculum levels**. This has prompted schools to think of a range of novel approaches to measure learner progress.[1]

As outlined in **Chapter 1**, assessment is the collection, judgement and processing of evidence for a designated educational purpose. In practice, this involves the collection and interpretation of data, typically in the form of scores. In this sense, data and assessment are natural bedfellows, and so it is unsurprising that all educational institutions are looking to maximise the potential for assessment-related data to inform educational decisions.

While assessment data are relatively easy to collect, and there are various sophisticated software programmes that facilitate their storage and management, it is a highly complex process to ensure the *quality* of the assessment data. At their best, assessment data can allow sound inferences to be made about students, measure progress, and personalise instruction. However, unfocused collection of assessment data can lead to burdens on educational practitioners, confusion of interpretation, and incorrect understanding of what learners know and can do.

There is an opportunity cost associated with the introduction of different approaches to assessment design, data analysis, and management. It is therefore essential that assessment practitioners first define the purposes and intended uses for their assessments so that investigations into the quality of assessment-derived data can focus on the degree to which the assessments meet those purposes.

Although assessment data can also be used for evaluation and improvement at the school or systemic level, the skills required for gathering and interpreting school- or programme-level data are quite different from those required for classroom assessment.[2] The focus of this chapter is on using assessment data for the purpose of informing teaching and learning. To meet this aim, we outline three foci for using assessment data effectively at the learner or classroom level:

1. understanding assessment data quality;
2. measuring progress;
3. reaching appropriate conclusions.

FOCUS 1: UNDERSTANDING ASSESSMENT DATA QUALITY

In **Chapter 2**, validation was introduced as a fundamental concept in determining the quality of an assessment. Validation is the collection of empirical evidence in order to support or refute the claims that you want to make about learners based on their assessment performance. The appropriate validation of assessment is vital in supporting the decisions or judgments that you want to derive from assessment data. Shaw and Crisp's framework (Table 2.2 in **Chapter 2**) highlighted several important questions when considering the quality of assessment and identifying any subsequent threats to validity. This brings us to an important first point about utilising assessment data for learning, instruction, or measuring progress – if the assessment quality itself is poor, then all subsequent analysis based on the assessment outcomes will have little value.

Before we can make claims about students with confidence, the assessments themselves need to be interrogated using the **qualitative** and/or **quantitative data** that are available to us.[3] We want to be sure that the assessment data outcomes (i.e. final scores or grades) are reliably representing ability related to the target construct. Qualitative data could come from the audit trail of assessment design and delivery, feedback from assessed participants, or feedback from other stakeholders. Quantitative data could be sourced from student performance at the item or assessment level, marking reliability data, or other data related to the processes underpinning standard-setting or -maintaining.

REFLECTION

What qualitative and/or quantitative data do you have available to you to evaluate the quality of your assessments?
Examples may include:

- documentary evidence (e.g. curriculum-mapping documents, assessment specifications, assessment development audit trails);
- evidence from practitioners (e.g. teacher feedback);
- evidence from stakeholders (e.g. student feedback, parental feedback, other enquiries about assessment outcomes);
- statistical performance of assessment-takers (assessment and item level);
- marking reliability statistics;
- correlations of scores between assessments.

PRACTICAL BOX 8.1

CLASSICAL TEST STATISTICS TO ANALYSE ASSESSMENT QUALITY

There are several quantitative analyses that can be conducted which give practitioners useful information about how well their assessment has functioned. Some commonly used and easily calculated examples are given below. These statistics are derived from **classical test theory (CTT)** – also known as 'true score theory' – and have been used to identify issues with assessments and items.

Mark distributions are plots of the scores achieved at either the item or assessment level. These plots provides an overview of assessment performance. The distribution of scores desired by the assessment developer may differ depending on the purpose of the assessment. For example, developers of large-scale summative assessments are usually aiming to create a normally distributed 'U-shaped' curve of scores. Assessment developers who are looking to check for mastery may expect a tighter distribution of marks towards the higher end of the scoring scale.

Standard deviation is the average distance from the mean score achieved on the assessment. It is closely related to the mark distribution and gives an indication of 'spread' of the scores achieved. The standard deviation gives a sense for how well the assessment or item is discriminating among the students. Low standard deviations indicate that the assessment-takers are 'bunched' around the mean. This makes it difficult to tell with certainty who is better on the topics covered in the assessment.

Omission rate is the proportion of assessment-takers who did not attempt an item. Omission rates above 0.05 indicate that something about the item might be problematic (e.g. the item was too difficult, or the assessment was too long for the time given).

Facility value is the mean mark achieved on an item divided by the maximum mark available. For single-mark items such as single-response multiple-choice questions, this is the proportion of assessment-takers who answered correctly. For example, a facility value of 0.5 indicates that assessment-takers achieved an average of 50 per cent of the marks available. High facility values indicate an easy item and low facility values indicate a difficult item. As a general rule, items with facility values above 0.75 or below 0.25 can be problematic. This is because the items are reducing the discriminative power of the overall assessment. Facility values need to be considered alongside the intended demand for the item. If, for example, you were expecting the item to be of low demand but ended up having a low facility value, it may indicate an issue with the item.

Discrimination indices provide evidence about whether the questions discriminate between good students and weak ones. One discrimination index correlates test scores on the item with the score on the whole assessment (known as the 'R_total'). A similar calculation (known as the 'R_rest') correlates the scores on the item with the score on the whole assessment, *but not including the item itself.*

The possible range of the discrimination indices is −1.0 to 1.0. Positive values indicate that students who did well on the item also did well on the overall assessment. Negative values indicate that students who performed well overall did badly on the item (or that students who did not perform well overall did well on the item). A discrimination index of 0.20 or above is usually thought to be acceptable.

The facility value and discrimination indices are linked. If an item has a very high or very low facility, the potential value of your chosen discrimination index will be much less than if the item has a mid-range facility. Another way of thinking about this would be that if there was a question which everyone got either correct or incorrect, there would be no way of knowing which students were better or worse on the topic that the assessment was covering.

Item characteristic curves (ICCs) are a plot of the facility values that are presented after the students have been split into groups. One way to do this is by using the quartiles of the total test score. ICCs can help to reveal if there are any biases in the question (for further discussion on assessment bias, see **Chapter 4**). Let us look at an example of an ICC in Figure 8.1.

(Continued)

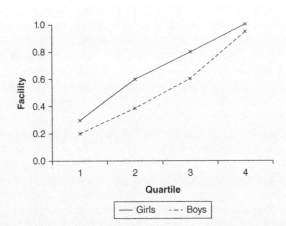

Figure 8.1 Example of an item characteristic curve

Figure 8.1 suggests that as the ability of the students increases (as represented by their quartile), the facility value also increases. However, boys appear to be performing worse than girls for quartiles 1 to 3. This indicates that there might be something contained in this item which is causing boys to underperform relative to girls. This could be related to the contextualisation of the item or to their understanding of what the item is asking them to do. Interestingly, the higher-performing boys are performing as well as girls, which suggests that the bias can be overcome.

These statistics are easily calculated, as well as providing useful information to understand both performance on the assessment and whether the assessment itself has performed according to expectations. Although these statistics have been widely used, a limitation is that they are somewhat dependent on the particulars of the sample from which you have collected data. It is not possible, for example, to conclude from these statistics by themselves whether you have a particularly strong or weak cohort of students. This issue may not be particularly relevant where successive cohorts are reasonably representative and do not vary across time. To check the comparability of different cohorts, more complex statistical procedures may be required, such as item response theory (IRT).[4]

FOCUS 2: MEASURING PROGRESS

If you are confident that your assessment is providing an appropriate degree of challenge and 'assessing the right things', it then becomes possible to explore assessment data in a meaningful way. Educators often want to know the degree of progress that learners are making, either within a lesson, across a set period of learning (e.g. a term, a semester) or in relation to curriculum outcomes. 'Progress' is defined as the development towards a more advanced condition, and educators are often looking for assessment to demonstrate improvements in learners as they go through their education.

The first challenge for educators is the process of defining the 'more advanced condition' to build towards. Curriculum and learning outcomes, grade statements, competency definitions, and assessment criteria can contribute to the definition. Educators develop a sense for what the 'end point' of attainment is, and then build curriculum and assessment models that aim to scaffold learners to the end state.

A second challenge is setting the conditions for student attainment and progress to be tracked effectively while also supporting teaching and learning practice. One approach that has proven popular in the UK is the use of *flight paths*. Flight paths have become common practice in schools since the removal of national curriculum levels. Teachers were looking for ways to represent progress between the beginning and end of schooling. The idea of flight paths is that they use outcomes from formal standardised assessments around the beginning of a stage of learning and use national data to arrive at a prediction for attainment at the end of that stage of learning. At each subsequent substage (e.g. at the end of a school term), there is a further prediction of 'expected progress' at that stage for each individual student, using the 'currency' of the final grading framework. There are many variations on this idea, but a typical simplified example is shown in Table 8.1 to represent expected progress from the beginning of Key Stage 3 (Year 7, age 10–11) to the end of Key Stage 4 (Year 11, age 15–16).

Table 8.1   Example of flight path data dashboard

Student	KS2 score	GCSE grade prediction	Year 8 'grade'	GCSE grade trajectory	Progress
A	118	8+	4+	8–	Below expectations
B	114	7+	4+	8–	Above expectations
C	104	5+	2=	5+	Meeting expectations

These flight path data use the relationship between assessment outcomes gathered at the end of primary school (Key Stage 2) with later GCSE outcomes at Key Stage 4. This provides a prediction of student performance up to five years in the future. Assessment data are then collected in an attempt to map individual learners' progress towards the end goal set for them.

The use of flight paths for tracking progress has been criticised for several reasons. The first issue is that it is not possible to make a direct link between the grades at the end of a Key Stage (such as GCSE grades) and student progress in the years preceding it. There is a disconnect between the use of a grade (which has been designed to represent a level of attainment at, for example, the end of Key Stage 4) and classroom practice. In-class assessments, aside from mock examinations which occur in close proximity to a final summative assessment, do not cover the entirety of the curriculum or syllabus that is targeted in GCSE assessment. In-class, end of term, or end-of-year assessments are instead focused on specifics of the curriculum that may be revisited at different times and in more complex ways. It is therefore not possible to extrapolate what performance on an in-class assessment means in terms of a GCSE grade.

A second issue is that referencing final grade outcomes at earlier educational stages implies an unrealistic degree of predictive precision. David Didau summarised this point as follows:

> If I'm given a GCSE grade, what I'm being told is that the teacher has the power to forecast the future and determine not only how well my child will do in an examination at some, possibly distant, point in the future, but that the teacher can also predict how well they're likely to do in relation to every other child who takes the exam. This is intellectually dishonest.[5]

The main point here is that progress is not linear as represented by flight path models. Attaching a pseudo-grade to children as they move through school potentially masks more fine-grained information that could otherwise be gleaned from assessments.

Third, and related to the second point, predictions between key stages are useful at the national level but not at the student level because of natural variation. There is also the issue that in most subjects, there is often no prior attainment data available in the subject discipline on which to base predictions. This means that the target grades produced have an illusion of precision.

Finally, student knowledge of their position on the flight path can be demotivating. If a student is told in their second year of schooling that they are predicted a specific grade four years in the future and that they are on course to do so according to their assessment performance, this may cap their aspirations for higher attainment. This goes against the idea of the 'growth mindset', which is dependent on the holding the belief that effort, persistence and the embracing of challenges can lead to future successes (see **Chapter 12**).

PRINCIPLES FOR USING ASSESSMENT DATA TO TRACK PROGRESS

For the reasons above, the use of flight paths has proved controversial. Assessment data are being used by schools to map onto grade outcomes in imprecise and inconsistent ways. There indeed appears to be an epidemic of over-extrapolation. Schools assess students at various times, targeting the knowledge, skills and understanding appropriate to their curriculum progress. However, from these assessments, predictive judgements are made with reference to a grading framework that has little meaning until very late in schooling. Furthermore, although learning progress is by its nature non-linear, the use of flight paths encourages a fixation where students are on a linear increase in 'altitude'. This might be visually appealing on a programme dashboard but of little use to teachers, who will inevitably need to drill down into the assessment data at fine-grained levels to truly establish what their next teaching interventions should be.

How should assessment data be utilised in schools and other educational institutions to measure progress? Below we suggest three principles to follow. Overall, these principles are underpinned by the idea that teachers should be as precise as possible in establishing why the data are being collected and their a priori limitations, as well as resisting the temptation to over-extrapolate the data in terms of what they predict.

DETERMINE THE USES FOR ASSESSMENT-RELATED DATA AND REPORTS

The primary aim of using assessment data to track progress is to have a sound understanding of the purpose of individual assessments, understand what comparisons are appropriate (e.g. between performance on one test and another), and make sound inferences that inform teaching and instruction.

Dylan Wiliam has argued that the collection and interpretation of assessment data should either aim to inform the teacher about the next learning steps or cause children 'to think'[6] (for a further discussion, see **Chapter 12**). This is particularly important when it comes to reporting and feedback. For example, if a raw score on an end-of-term assessment is converted to a flight path indicator (e.g. *meeting expectations* based on alignment to a grade on the flight path), one has to consider what teachers, learners or parents would be able to *do* with that information in terms of teaching interventions or strategies. If the outcomes for diligently recording and manipulating large swathes of data do not contribute to these outcomes, then it is reducing the amount of available teaching time that could be focused on more useful things.

CONSIDER PROGRESS AT THE CURRICULUM LEVEL

The focus of collecting assessment data should be to demonstrate the degree to which learners are successfully moving through the curriculum. There are several possible ways that this can be done, two of which are listed below:

Progress related to a topic: Topic assessments before and after a period of learning can establish the security of the knowledge and understanding within an individual lesson. Assessment data are representative of the journey to mastery for individual topics. What is important to note here is that the topics themselves may have different levels of challenge for learners, and so it may not be productive to compare directly between topic tests. It is therefore essential for educators to hold a 'standard' in mind where they can be secure that a learner or group of learners hold a sufficient degree of mastery.

Trajectory through the curriculum: If, over a series of topic assessments, students are showing increasing mastery of the topics, then this is a sound indicator that they are progressing through the curriculum. Daisy Christodoulou, in her book *Making Good Progress?*, suggested that assessments which are designed to confirm key knowledge and understanding (e.g. multiple-choice tests) can be a precursor to more formalised assessments that more closely resemble the final learning outcomes identified at the end of a Key Stage.[7] In this approach, movement through the curriculum is based on the gradual synthesis of component knowledge, skills and understanding that eventually contribute to the desired end state. The use of curriculum statements can be useful here to set the particular parameters to shape assessment tasks, as well as contributing towards an agreed curriculum progression model.

UTILISE PROFESSIONAL JUDGEMENT

If the purpose for using assessment-related data is to understand the degree to which students have moved towards a desired state, as well as informing the next steps for moving towards that end state, then teacher judgement is an important part of that process. Assessment data need to be interrogated for anomalies and trends that may be indicative of progress being made or any emerging issues. For example, you may want to look at individual item-level performance related to a topic where you are unsure as to whether learners have grasped the concept. You may also want to analyse the relative position of students from one assessment to the next to pick up any unusual patterns in performance.

FOCUS 3: REACHING APPROPRIATE CONCLUSIONS FOR INSTRUCTION

Assessment data can be presented in myriad ways using numerous computer programmes and software. There is an opportunity cost in the recording and interpretation of assessment-related data. The presentation (or re-presentation) of assessment data only reaches utility once educators can: (a) understand and interpret the information presented to them; and (b) have the opportunity to use the information to inform appropriate conclusions and subsequent actions.

Helen Timperley outlined five conditions for assessment data to be used effectively for teaching and learning:

- Assessment-related data need to be relevant to the outlined curriculum.
- Assessment-related data need to be perceived by educators as something that informs teaching and learning, rather than for accountability.
- Educators require knowledge of assessment data to make appropriate adjustments to practice.
- Educators require **pedagogical content knowledge** to make good adjustments to practice.
- Educators need to have opportunities to engage in cycles of inquiry to build knowledge and skills in assessment data.[8]

The first three points relate to educators' understanding of data and their underlying beliefs about how data can inform their practice. Teachers who are data-literate are able to utilise both assessment-related data and other data sourced from national, school and classroom levels in a manner appropriate to their roles and responsibilities. Data literacy is necessarily supported by both content knowledge and pedagogical content knowledge. Ellen Mandinach and Edith Gummer suggest five elements of data literacy to inform teaching and learning:

- Identify a problem of practice related to a learner, classroom, curriculum or aspect of teaching.
- Use data that are appropriate to the identified problem.
- Transform data to information through appropriate interpretation of data, effective data representations, and understanding of causality.
- Transform information into a decision related to next instructional steps.
- Evaluate outcomes of the decisions reached from data collection and analysis.[9]

The final two elements taken together suggest a cycle of inquiry where educators use the assessment data available to them to monitor student performance, diagnose learner needs, make subsequent instructional adjustments that are sensitive to the educational context, and then re-examine the original issue raised by the data related to progress or attainment. Repeated cycles of inquiry build educators' understanding, questioning and criticality of the data that they analyse to inform their decision-making.

FINAL THOUGHTS

There are numerous pressures driving the requirement for schools and other education institutions to collect and interpret assessment data. Data understanding and management are increasingly becoming important parts of teachers' day-to-day practice and conceptualisations of competence. Teachers are required to justify their decision-making using 'hard' data rather than intuition or personal preferences.

A first focus for supporting assessment data literacy is to ascertain the degree to which individual assessments and items are fit for purpose. Only then can teachers have sufficient security of inference to be able to plan later teacher interventions. This data literacy at the 'micro' level will support broader considerations of how data are best analysed at the 'macro' level, such as in a department or across a school.

In this chapter, we have highlighted the use of flight paths as a potentially unhelpful way to convert assessment data for interpretation. Instead, we argue for a more curriculum-focused approach to assessment data collection and management. This approach affords a closer connection between the information provided by the data and the decision-making and subsequent evaluation in the classroom.

KEY TAKEAWAYS

- The collection and analysis of assessment data are important aspects of validation. Qualitative or quantitative data from a variety of different sources inform the degree to which you can support the claims you wish to make about assessment-takers.
- School assessment and data policies should focus on and encourage student engagement with curriculum content and outcomes.
- Assessment data literacy comprises several components, including identifying issues with assessment quality, transforming data into information that supports decision-making, and evaluating how data are being used.

9

ASSESSING COMMUNITY ACTION AND SERVICE

IN THIS CHAPTER, YOU WILL:

- review skills that are commonly listed as being important in the 21st century;
- see how some programmes run in schools and by external organisations give adolescents the opportunity to get involved in community action and service;
- reflect on the challenges of assessing action and service.

In the early 2000s, it was hard to read an article or attend a conference about education without reference to so-called 21st-century skills. Various lists were compiled, especially across Australia, Europe, the UK and the USA. Sometimes they were sponsored by large tech companies; perhaps unsurprisingly, many of them emphasised the importance of digital literacy or information and communications technology (ICT) literacy. Irenka Suto, in her aptly titled article '21st Century Skills: Ancient, Ubiquitous, Enigmatic?', summarised into four categories what she had found in the literature on the topic[1] and mapped onto them the ten skills listed by one of the most commonly quoted frameworks defined by the ATC21s project, headquartered at the University of Melbourne (see Table 9.1).[2]

Table 9.1   Four categories of 21st-century skills

Ways of thinking	Creativity and innovation
	Critical thinking, problem-solving, decision-making
	Learning to learn, metacognition
Ways of working	Communication
	Collaboration (teamwork)
Tools for working	Information literacy (including research on sources, evidence, biases, etc.)
	ICT literacy
Living in the world	Citizenship – local and global
	Life and career
	Personal and social responsibility (including cultural awareness and competence)

Some commentators talked about 21st-century skills to illustrate a break between what they saw as the more traditional education systems of the previous two centuries since mass schooling began and the digital era that was just beginning. They wanted students to know things but also know *how* to do things. Sometimes the 'knowing how' was termed as having 'soft skills', and these skills were – and still are   much sought after by many employers across professions.

Andreas Schleicher, the division head and coordinator of the OECD Programme for International Student Assessment (PISA) and the OECD Indicators of Education Systems programme, caught the zeitgeist when he wrote:

> A generation ago, teachers could expect that what they taught would last their students a lifetime. Today, because of rapid economic and social change, schools have to pre-pare students for jobs that have not yet been created, technologies that have not yet been invented and problems that we don't yet know will arise.[3]

Putting aside the scope of digital technologies, it could be argued that each generation throughout history has had to adapt to the world as it evolves, but it could also be reasoned, as Schleicher goes on to say:

> The knowledge world is no longer divided between specialists and generalists. A new group – let's call them 'versatilists' – has emerged. They apply depth of skill to a pro-gressively widening scope of situations and experiences, gaining new competencies, building relationships and assuming new roles.[4]

It is the duty of teachers to help students learn about more than individual disciplines and to support them in making connections between and outside them. The curriculum offered nowadays by an excellent school is not just about subjects or subjects plus, for example, sports teams and arts clubs; it is about the whole 'experienced curriculum'.[5] It is often through the *whole* educational experience which a school offers, rather than in its prescribed range of courses, that students are able to access the situations and experiences which Schleicher writes about.

In this chapter, we are going to discuss how we assess the skills gained in extracurricular activities, such as community service and award-bearing programmes. We will exclude the expressive arts, as we dedicate **Chapter 11** to them, and we will also omit the assessment of sports ability, which in school-based syllabuses usually comprises a mix of theory and carefully defined performance levels relative to each sport.[6] We will also consider some of the challenges of assessing community action and service.

COMMUNITY ACTION AND SERVICE PROGRAMMES

In their mission statements, schools often talk about their place in the local, national and global community. They encourage and enable connections with the world beyond their boundaries by offering students opportunities to engage in and explore how they can make a difference. This might be through action groups, such as on environmental issues, by volunteering or through other forms of community service. The term 'community service' can sometimes have negative connotations as it can relate to unpaid work that offenders have to do instead of going to prison, but we of course mean it in its positive sense. The intended outcomes of community action and service are to develop a combination of knowledge, skills, values and motivation that students can bring back into their school lives and out into their current and future personas.

Some school programmes oblige students to undertake a determined amount of action and service. One such example is the International Baccalaureate (IB) Diploma Programme (DP). One of the three elements at the core of this programme (the others being an extended essay and a course called 'theory of knowledge') is creativity, action and service, commonly known by its acronym CAS. The IB describes CAS as being 'at the heart of the DP'.[7]

The three strands of CAS are defined as follows:

- *Creativity*: Exploring and extending ideas leading to an original or interpretive product or performance.
- *Action*: Physical exertion contributing to a healthy lifestyle.
- *Service*: Collaborative and reciprocal engagement with the community in response to an authentic need.[8]

CAS is about more than a list of singular, unconnected experiences. The IB describes students' service experiences as typically involving:

- Investigation, preparation and action that meets an identified need.
- Reflection on significant experiences throughout to inform problem-solving and choices.
- Demonstration, allowing for sharing of what has taken place.[9]

In other words, students are supported to plan and to find meaning in the actions that they are doing. Through this experience, it is intended that students will identify their own strengths and discover areas for growth, develop new skills, demonstrate commitment, understand the benefits of working with and for others without the expectation of reciprocation or reward, and learn to evaluate the impact of their actions.

Throughout their two-year DP, students – with the guidance of a coordinator in their school – maintain and complete a portfolio as evidence of what they have done and what they have learned. They should demonstrate in their portfolio that they have achieved each of the seven learning outcomes prescribed by the IB at least once and reflected upon them. The school then informs the IB that each student has fulfilled this aspect of the DP's core. It is the *school's* ability to oversee a meaningful CAS programme that is assessed by the IB, rather than the students' individual work.

Mary Hayden and colleagues, in their study of the impact of CAS on students and communities, stated that 'participation in creativity, action, service (CAS) was perceived to contribute to changes in Diploma Programme (DP) students in terms of their personal dispositions, behaviour and interpersonal relationships'.[10] They also underlined that schools need to prepare students to understand why doing CAS is a valuable use of their time, as well as the importance of setting goals before starting an activity. Shona McIntosh, in her subsequent research, also suggested that students are more likely to benefit in their learning if there is an 'intentionally-educational purpose' behind their activities, and that how well a CAS programme is run and resourced is highly influential on its success.[11] We will return to this latter point later in the chapter when we consider the challenges of assessing action and service.

The absence of examined or external assessment is also the case in syllabuses such as Singapore's character and citizenship evaluation (CCE) course.[12] The course was designed to develop students holistically, and their completion of it is evaluated through a range of internal assessment models, including self-assessment, peer assessment and teachers' reports. In the US, the National Assessment of Educational Progress (NAEP), a research division of the Department of Education, assesses a sample of students on a number of subjects, including civics, which is taken as a course in some states. Part of this assessment is based on students' responses to a series of multiple-choice, short-response and extended-response questions.[13] The latter give students the opportunity to discuss, for example, not only what they can do for their local community, but how and why. Students' learning can thus go deeper and involve aspects of critical and creative thinking.

AWARD-BEARING PROGRAMMES

One of the most celebrated programmes for 14–24-year-olds is the Duke of Edinburgh's (DofE) International Award, which began in the 1950s. The programme was conceived to bridge the gap between the end of formal education (age 15 at the time in the UK) and national service (for men at the age of 18). It was set up 'so that young men made the best use of their free time, found interests and acquired self-confidence and a sense of purpose that would support them into their future and help them to become well-rounded citizens'.[14] It has grown since then to include girls and young women, and is offered in 130 countries and territories, with some 300,000 individuals worldwide now starting a DofE programme each year. The DofE programme can be offered either by schools or external organisations.

There are three progressive levels of award: bronze, silver and gold. There are four sections to complete in each of the first two levels (volunteering, physical, skills, expedition), with the addition of a fifth for gold (residential). These days, the DofE programme is described as a way for young people to:

> have fun, make friends, improve their self-esteem and build confidence. They gain essential skills and attributes for work and life such as resilience, problem-solving, team-working, communication and drive, enhancing CVs and university and job applications.[15]

Under the guidance of supervisors, award participants plan and undertake activities that enable them to demonstrate new learning, including self-belief and self-confidence, a sense of identity, initiative-taking and responsibility, and how to collaborate and communicate with others.

In common with the IB CAS programme, of which the DofE Award is sometimes part, there is no formal assessment of individual achievement against criteria. Appointed assessors, using guidance and report forms, check on individual participants' contribution, development and progress, as well as agreeing the completion of a planned section of the programme. Assessors are advised to 'celebrate the achievement of the young person' and to keep comments 'personal, positive and encouraging'.[16]

REFLECTION

Programmes such as the DofE and CAS are devised to provide young people with many opportunities and routes to learn, demonstrate and gain recognition for a range of 'soft' or '21st-century' skills. Take a look again at the descriptions of CAS and DofE, and consider the claims being made about the programmes and how they are assessed.
   What, in your opinion, is the *validity* of these claims?

A 2019 summary of research into the impact of the Duke of Edinburgh's International Award highlighted some of the favourable outcomes that participants enjoy, including greater prospects for employment and well-being, a propensity to respect diversity and interact socially with people from different backgrounds, and – with regard to the rehabilitation of young offenders – an increase in self-esteem. It also states that in 2015, the award was chosen by human resources professionals in a survey that asked what they considered to be the most recognised volunteering programme during the recruitment process of new candidates.[17]

CHALLENGES IN ASSESSING COMMUNITY ACTION AND SERVICE

As we have seen throughout this chapter and elsewhere in this book (e.g. see **Chapter 7**), action and service in their various forms are not often assessed by formal examination. Those presenting themselves for assessment to obtain an award or qualification either do so by a portfolio of evidence or observation by an expert practitioner who may be a mentor. There is often an element of reflection either in- or on-action; and for elements of programmes such as the IB Diploma, it is this that counts more than the number of hours accumulated.

In programmes where students have to write answers to extended-response questions, they often also have to consider hypothetical situations. This can address issues of equity, as some students may have had more opportunities than others to participate in community service. The same is true of all the activities that we have described in this chapter. A student's success may be dependent on the type of institution that they attend, its extended curriculum, its teachers, coordinators, leaders, and maybe also their family background.

And where opportunities are available, a student's motivation to succeed may depend on how seriously they take this element of their education. Research suggests that teachers perceive summative assessment generally to be a useful tool; and that in schools where extracurricular subjects or activities focusing on actions and skills were not formally assessed, students may question their value.[18]

The contexts in which students are having to be creative, communicative and collaborative, as well as thinking critically or metacognitively, can be quite different when they are performing community service activities compared to when they are in formal lessons at school. They reveal very different interpretations of what it means to be effective in how you act or think, as well as creating challenges in defining what is 'good'. The assessment of these areas is therefore often directly linked to discipline knowledge and other foundational capacities. It is hard to consider soft skills in isolation.

FINAL THOUGHTS

Towards the end of the 20th century, UNESCO released a seminal report called *Learning: The Treasure Within*.[19] This document, which might be seen as having laid the foundations for the lists of 21st-century skills, underlined the fundamental role that education has to play in personal and social development, as well as the individual's responsibility to play a role in the progress of their community. The report established four 'pillars of education', set out in Table 9.2.

Table 9.2   The four pillars of education

Learning to know	By combining a sufficiently broad general knowledge with the opportunity to work in depth on a small number of subjects.
	This also means learning to learn so as to benefit from the opportunities that education provides throughout life.
Learning to do	In order to acquire not only an occupational skill, but also – more broadly – the competence to deal with many situations and work in teams.
	It also means learning to do in the context of young people's various social and work experiences, which may be informal (as a result of the local or national context) or formal (involving courses, alternating study and work).

| Learning to live together, learning to live with others | By developing an understanding of other people and an appreciation of interdependence – carrying out joint projects and learning to manage conflicts – in a spirit of respect for the values of pluralism, mutual understanding and peace. |
| Learning to be | So as to better develop one's personality and be able to act with ever-greater autonomy, judgement and personal responsibility. In that connection, education must not disregard any aspect of a person's potential: memory, reasoning, aesthetic sense, physical capacities and communication skills. |

Whether or not 'some skills are too subjective and enigmatic to be measured objectively',[20] they may describe in a common language a set of standards for how to conduct ourselves in life in whatever forms of community action and service we pursue.

KEY TAKEAWAYS

- Some employers value certain skills more in the 21st-century; education organisations have responded by providing opportunities for students to gain them.
- Many schools organise activities, such as community service, either as part of the curriculum or extra to it; other organisations offer young people programmes to obtain awards that showcase the volunteering or practical and social skills which they have gained.
- Few programmes that promote student action are formally assessed other than through portfolios and observation, but meaningful planning and reflection are key aspects of meeting success criteria.
- It is challenging to assess action and service in isolation because it is subjective, depends on the opportunities given to students, and is integral both to other subjects within a curriculum and to playing an active role in society.

10

ASSESSING COLLABORATION

IN THIS CHAPTER, YOU WILL:

- learn about the importance and challenges of assessing collaboration effectively;
- consider how the assessment of collaboration can be optimised by using four 'decision points' as an operational framework.

Although collaboration has been identified as a so-called 21st-century skill (for a description of this term, see **Chapter 9**), it is something that has evolutionary roots. Humans share cognitive, social and physical resources from a very young age, but our nearest primate relatives do so only in very restricted ways.[1] One of the reasons for the success of *Homo sapiens* as a species is that they have cognitive mechanisms to coordinate activities with partners, as well as methods to ensure that individual participants in collaborative activity each benefit sufficiently to incentivise group coordination.[2] Collaboration is something that is a hardwired element of the human condition.

The deep-rooted importance of collaboration to the functioning of society, as well as the more recent identification of collaboration skills as being an educational outcome in its own right,[3] has led to debates about how it can be optimally assessed. Collaboration's status as a 21st-century skill has been reaffirmed in recent years by the growing emphasis on project- and enquiry-based learning, as well as the increasing requirement for learners to demonstrate their knowledge in social settings. Projects such as the Partnership for 21st Century Skills[4] and the Organisation for Economic Co-operation and Development's (OECD) recent assessment for collaborative problem-solving[5] have heightened the need to consider how the assessment of collaboration can be operationalised and optimised – what has been labelled the 'assessment imperative'.[6]

In this chapter, we first explore the difficulties in assessing collaboration effectively and then look at some pragmatic steps for assessment developers to consider. The first question to ask is: Why is collaboration so difficult to conceptualise and measure?

WHY IS COLLABORATION 'HARD TO MEASURE'?

The first and most fundamental challenge for the assessment of collaboration is that although we may observe good examples of collaborative activity in day-to-day life, collaboration remains a vague concept that is intimately tied to contextual scenarios.[7]

For example, imagine a group of children in a playground. On one side of the playground, you see some children sitting in a circle with some toys (what we will call group 1), while on the other side you see children playing a game of football (group 2). How would you know if any of the individuals in either group were collaborating well with each other? In both cases, you would likely be looking for behavioural cues to determine that the children are engaging in and maintaining a joint activity. For group 1, you may be looking to observe particular behavioural cues (e.g. joint attention, references to others) and actions that aim to maintain the 'rules' of the pretend play scenario (e.g. keeping to assigned roles). For group 2, however, the cues you may be looking for could be very different. In a game of football, the rules are commonly understood by participants, and so the focus of your observation may be on how conflicts are resolved or how individual players contribute to the outcome of the game (i.e. the final score).

A second challenge for assessing collaboration is that it is difficult to isolate individuals' contributions to the collaborative endeavour among the 'noise' created by different group compositions.[8] This issue is particularly important when we consider that assessment scores or grades are usually reported at the individual level. There have been recent attempts to improve the record-keeping of collaborative interactions using technology, such as the recording of group work using multiple cameras.[9] Solutions such as this increase the opportunity to revisit and refocus on individuals' contributions. However, it can significantly increase the load for assessors to process, code and reliably judge the quality of the interactions according to the set criteria. Other technological approaches have attempted to standardise the collaborative scenarios that individuals are confronted with by using computer-simulated collaborative partners.[10] For this approach, a computer agent initiates collaborative behaviour but occasionally 'tests' the learner by displaying some misunderstandings or suggesting misleading strategies. At this point, the learner must negotiate and resolve the conflict with the computer.

A third challenge is that to contribute effectively to a collaboration, group members need to have a sufficient degree of knowledge, skills and understanding related to the set task. For example, if the collaboration involved the design of a new cantilever bridge, then individual group members would need to have discipline knowledge in the fields of mathematics, physics, structural engineering and/or architectural design in order to contribute effectively. This makes it important for assessors of collaboration to set tasks that are accessible to all group members.

HOW DO WE ASSESS COLLABORATION EFFECTIVELY?

The challenges of assessing collaboration outlined above mean that it is necessary to develop a degree of precision at different stages of assessment development, while also being aware of important trade-offs in relation to construct validity, reliability and manageability (for more on the tensions between these three concepts, see **Chapter 3**). In terms of making secure inferences about a learner's capacities in collaboration, it is important to make decisions regarding how collaboration is to be conceptualised, how the evidence produced will be used to make judgements, how the assessment can be designed to facilitate collaboration among group members, and how credit among the assessment-takers will be distributed. We explore each of these 'decision points' in turn below.

DECISION POINT 1: DEFINE THE CONSTRUCT OF COLLABORATION

The first step in operationalising the assessment of collaboration is to develop an understanding of the key facets of collaborative activity. The OECD suggested that collaboration can be defined as:

> the capacity of an individual to effectively engage in a process whereby *two or more agents* attempt to *solve a problem* by *sharing the understanding and effort* required to come to a solution and pooling their knowledge, skills and efforts to reach that solution.[11] [emphasis added]

Looking at the first emphasised part of this definition ('two or more agents'), it makes intuitive sense that for collaboration to occur, two or more people need to be working together in some capacity. The second emphasised element ('solve a problem') has important implications for assessors as there has to be a sufficiently complex problem that the collaborators can work on together (see decision point 3). The third emphasised element ('sharing the understanding and effort') refers to the maintenance of a collaborative 'state' (i.e. the group agreeing to work on the set problem together).[12]

Simon Child and Stuart Shaw expanded on the OECD's definition to identify two components of the collaborative process: *collaborative 'state' maintenance* and *socio-cognitive behaviours*.[13,14] 'State' maintenance comprises behaviours and actions that mediate the joint effort inherent to collaboration. Socio-cognitive behaviours build knowledge and understanding through linguistic exchanges that have been defined by the nature of the collaborative task. Each component can be further divided into three interrelated facets, which are briefly defined in Table 10.1.

Table 10.1 Components of the collaborative process

Component of the collaborative process	Facet	Definition
Collaborative 'state' maintenance	Maintaining positive social interdependence	Individuals working to maintain the group's motivation to work together, as well as the belief that the group is greater than the sum of its parts.
	Communication	The rich interactive features, of which only one is the speech (or text) produced by group members. Communication acts to bring implicit thought to the surface.
	Cooperation	The division of labour among group members. Cooperation occurs when aspects of a task are divided up into manageable subparts that can be achieved by individuals.
Socio-cognitive behaviours	Conflict resolution	Group interaction promotes cognitive conflict by exposing discrepancies between group members' own and others' knowledge. Conflict resolution relates to the negotiation and subsequent consensus of decision-making.
	Introduction of new ideas	The offering of solutions for the task at hand, which can then be negotiated.
	Sharing of resources	The pooling of cognitive and/or physical resources among group members.

DECISION POINT 2: THE FOCUS OF THE ASSESSMENT – PROCESS OR OUTCOME

The next decision point for the assessment of collaboration is to decide upon the focus of the assessment. There are two main potential areas of focus: assessing the *quality of student interactions* (i.e. the process – see decision point 1) and the *quality of the group output* (i.e. the outcome).[15]

The focus on the *processes* that underpin effective collaboration is reflected in recent conceptualisations of 21st-century skills.[16] The components outlined by Child and Shaw above provide a way of conceptualising facets of the collaborative process. The key challenge for assessors is to collect sufficient observational data in order to judge how effectively individual students are contributing to the collaborative effort. As mentioned above, technology is potentially useful in this area. Technology can be used to keep a record of interactions (e.g. through video recording or audit logs),[17] and can also be used to simulate a collaborative partner.[18]

A focus on collaborative *outcomes* acknowledges that collaborative activity is working towards a resolution with respect to a defined problem. Collaborative groups typically have a goal for their activity, and assessors can judge the quality of the outcome reached. For example, if a group of students have been tasked with researching a previously unknown topic together, an assessor could judge a final outcome of a joint presentation or a co-written research paper. This can be pragmatically useful in circumstances where it is not possible to observe the students while they are undertaking the collaborative process. However, a risk of focusing on the quality of the outcome is that it could encourage less than optimal individual behaviours such as 'freeriding' or 'social loafing' in individuals,[19] particularly if the marks awarded are shared among group members (see decision point 4).

DECISION POINT 3: SETTING AN APPROPRIATE COLLABORATIVE TASK

For collaboration to be encouraged, and thus observable, it is important that the task itself should enable all group members to share their views and ideas on potential courses of action. Child and Shaw suggested four characteristics of an effectively set collaborative task:

The task should be sufficiently complex: This is important as it encourages group members to conduct research, and discuss potential solutions and courses of action. Simplistic or trivial tasks do not encourage group members to collaborate because there is little need to share resources, either cognitive or physical.

The task should be non-structured: Task complexity is determined in part by the structure provided when the task is set. Tasks should be sufficiently open so that the course of action has to be negotiated. Group members should also be asked to define individual group member roles themselves rather than having them defined by the assessor.

Group member dynamics engender negotiation: The socio-cognitive elements of the collaborative process are less likely to be observable if all group members immediately agree on the solution to a problem, or if one group member dominates the collaborative interaction. Where possible, the assessor should make sure that individual group members have differing perspectives or views which can be negotiated.

Group members should be motivated to work together: In setting the task, the assessor needs to motivate group members to work together. If the criteria outlined above are met, then the group dynamic and the task itself are likely to be highly motivating. Research has found that productivity is improved when members are rewarded as a group, within a context of individual accountability.[20,21]

This brings us to the final decision point: the distribution of marks.

DECISION POINT 4: DISTRIBUTION OF MARKS

The notion of reward structures on a collaborative task is closely related to the challenges of obtaining individual scores based on group activity. Focusing on the outcomes of collaborative group work leaves open the possibility for individual contributions (either good or bad) to be obscured. This may introduce potential unfairness to group members who would have benefited if their individual contributions to the group task were acknowledged. Giving individual scores related to each group member's contributions is more aligned to typical assessment purposes and practice but de-emphasises the fact that collaborative activities are goal-based. Collaborative activity should value both individual and group endeavour, and this should be reflected in the distribution of marks. In practice, this would mean both a shared group mark based on the final outcome alongside a mark for each individual based on their personal contributions to the collaborative task.

FINAL THOUGHTS

The decision points discussed above highlight the fundamental role of the assessor in ensuring the optimal conditions for assessing collaboration. For example, there is a delicate balance of setting a sufficiently open or non-structured task while also ensuring that all group members can contribute. Furthermore, group member motivations for collaborating with others are directly influenced not just by their beliefs about how they can participate, but also their understanding of how their contributions will be rewarded. Before developing assessments of collaboration, assessors need to understand which facets of collaboration they are interested in targeting (e.g. process versus outcome) while also setting up appropriate and accessible tasks where assessment-takers feel confident and able to contribute.

Efforts from the OECD and others to increase task control (e.g. via the use of computer-based collaborate partners) and improve evidence collation using technology are still in their relative infancy. These solutions have promise but do not yet reduce the interpretive load on teachers or other assessors who are interested in understanding individuals' contributions to group endeavour at scale. The decision points above offer a pragmatic approach to assessing collaboration, as well as acting to raise awareness of tensions related to construct validity and manageability.

KEY TAKEAWAYS

- Collaboration has been identified as both something observable to be assessed and a mechanism for how learning can be achieved.
- The collaborative process includes both the maintenance of the collaborative 'state' and the socio-cognitive contributions that support task resolution.
- Technology can potentially support the assessment of collaboration by acting as a record-keeper or collaborative partner.

11

ASSESSING THE EXPRESSIVE ARTS

IN THIS CHAPTER, YOU WILL:

- learn more about the contents of expressive arts syllabuses and how they are assessed;
- explore the challenges of assessing the expressive arts;
- consider how it is possible to form an initial holistic perception of the quality of an artwork, as well as the importance of referencing agreed criteria to support this judgement.

Most of us at some point in our lives will have had a good-humoured argument with a friend or family member about whether an artwork, film or piece of music is of high quality. We will have our favourites and opinions about who deserves a prize or whether it is worth paying a lot of money for something. People older and younger than us, or from other cultural backgrounds, will have different tastes. Our own environment will probably have influenced why we like a certain decade, genre or movement.

Nolan Gasser, chief architect of the Music Genome Project and author of *Why You Like It: The Science and Culture of Musical Taste*, suggests that the seeds of our musical tastes are planted early in our lives.[1] Studies of infants show that they can recognise a deviation from what they are used to hearing and – to a certain extent – seeing. The cognitive psychologist and former music producer Daniel Levitin, in his book *This Is Your Brain on Music*, says:

> Musical preferences ... have a large social component based on our knowledge of the singer or musician, on our knowledge of what our family and friends like, and knowledge of what that music stands for.[2]

In other words, we form 'schemas' of what we like through our upbringing and personal learning experiences, so it is quite normal that 'what one person finds insipid and hideously simple, another person might find difficult to understand'.[3]

REFLECTION

See if you can describe what it is about a certain type or piece of music or art that you like.

What has influenced this preference? How do you react when you encounter something that you do not like? What unspoken or unwritten criteria have you developed that underpin your judgements?

In this chapter, we are going to explore how it is possible to step outside the bias of our schemas and formally assess the expressive arts. We will be looking at the issue from an academic rather than a critical perspective, although the latter will enter the discussion as well.

WHAT ARE THE EXPRESSIVE ARTS?

In the Welsh national curriculum, the 'Expressive Arts Area of Learning and Experience' includes the five disciplines of art, dance, drama, film and digital media, and music, and sets out three complementary 'statements of what matters':

- Exploring the expressive arts is essential to developing artistic skills and knowledge, and it enables learners to become curious and creative individuals.
- Responding and reflecting, both as artist and audience, is a fundamental part of learning in the expressive arts.
- Creating combines skills and knowledge, drawing on the senses, inspiration and imagination.[4]

Many educationalists underline the importance of maintaining an arts curriculum, both because those who have strengths in this area deserve the opportunity to showcase and be rewarded for their studies and dedication, and because of the extra dimension that the study or practice of the expressive arts brings to learning in other subject areas. Here is what one assessment organisation says:

A broad and balanced curriculum recognises that encouraging the arts can help students to develop their own creative voice and creative thinking skills. Studying an arts subject can also build learners' self-confidence as they feel valued for their unique contributions and talents.[5]

The distinction between the many expressive arts is a grey area, especially as genres develop and intermingle. In basic terms, 'visual arts' refers to artists using various materials to create physical or static art objects, whereas 'performing arts' refers to artists using inanimate objects and their own bodies and voices to express something in an artistic way.

VISUAL ARTS IN THE SCHOOL CURRICULUM

In whatever way we choose to categorise the expressive arts, key concepts, stages and expectations of learning have been established within each discipline in the shape of syllabuses or subject guides to enable us to review progress and assess attainment. Here are some examples from different assessment organisations to give you a flavour of what is involved in two visual arts disciplines. When you look through them, think back to the principles of assessment design that we discussed in **Part A** to see how what is outlined reflects them.

The aims of the Cambridge International AS and A level in art and design are to enable students to:

- develop an inquisitive, creative approach to research and problem-solving;
- develop the ability to record from first-hand observation, personal experience and other sources;
- effectively communicate their personal response by improving technical skills in a range of processes and media;
- develop independent expression by analysing, evaluating and applying concepts and techniques;
- articulate ideas and responses to their work and the work of others using a relevant vocabulary;
- develop a clear contextual framework that aids critical reflection of their work;
- develop a critical understanding of important concepts and formal elements of art and design;
- develop the skills needed to study art and design at higher education.[6]

Students can choose whether to focus on fine art, graphic communication, three-dimensional design, or textiles and fashion. Those who take the full A level are assessed in three components:

1. *Coursework*: Candidates research, develop and realise a project from one area of study in the syllabus content divided into two parts – a portfolio and a final outcome.
2. *Externally set assignment*: Candidates choose one starting point to develop into a personal response, which comprises supporting studies, created during the preparation period and a final outcome, produced during a supervised test of 15 hours' total duration.
3. *Personal investigation*: Candidates investigate a theme, idea, concept or process that is personal to them in the form of practical work and written analysis.

The aims of the IB Diploma film course are to enable students to:

- explore the various contexts of film and make links to – and between – films, film-makers and film-making techniques (*inquiry*);
- acquire and apply skills as discerning interpreters of film and as creators of film, working both individually and collaboratively (*action*).[7]

Students of the film course at higher level are assessed in four ways (the first two externally and the latter two internally):

1. *Textual analysis*: of a prescribed film text based on a chosen extract, and list of sources.
2. *Comparative study*: Recorded multimedia comparative study, and list of sources.
3. *Film portfolio*: including a list of sources and a film reel.
4. *Collaborative film project*: Completed film, project report and list of sources.

PERFORMING ARTS IN THE SCHOOL CURRICULUM

Here are some examples from different assessment organisations to give you a feel for what is involved in two performing arts disciplines. We will look at music in more detail when we consider the assessment of performance in broader terms.

The subject content of the AQA GCSE drama syllabus is divided into three components:

1. Understanding drama

   a. Knowledge and understanding of drama and theatre
   b. Study of one set play from a choice of six
   c. Analysis and evaluation of the work of live theatre makers
   – assessed by an open book written exam.

2. Devising drama

   a. Process of creating devised drama
   b. Performance of devised drama (students may contribute as performer or designer)
   c. Analysis and evaluation of own work
   – assessed by a devising log and a devised performance.

3. Texts in practice

   a. Performance of two extracts from one play (students may contribute as performer or designer)
   – assessed by performance of the two extracts.[8]

In the general senior syllabus for dance from the Queensland Curriculum and Assessment Authority in Australia, students learn about:

- *Moving bodies*: How does dance communicate meaning for different purposes and in different contexts?
- *Moving through environments*: How does the integration of the environment shape dance to communicate meaning?
- *Moving statements*: How is dance used to communicate viewpoints?
- *Moving my way*: How does dance communicate meaning for me?[9]

For this syllabus, the first three elements described below (75 per cent) are internally assessed and the last element (25 per cent) is externally assessed:

1. Students *perform* a contemporary dance devised by the teacher or a guest artist that involves students' application of identified skills.
2. Students *choreograph* a dance that communicates a social, political or cultural viewpoint. The purpose of the dance is to challenge and provoke the audience.
3. Students create a dance work to communicate a personal viewpoint in response to selected stimulus in the form of a *project*.
4. Students analyse, interpret and evaluate information in the development of a response to an unseen stimulus and an unseen question in a *written mode*.

REFLECTION

If you were not previously aware of the aims and assessment methods for expressive arts courses, is there anything that surprises you in what we have outlined above in our four examples? What (if anything) strikes you as being different about the study of these subjects compared to others that you know? What advantages and challenges can you see in teaching and assessing the expressive arts?

Readers who have not previously looked at how the expressive arts are assessed may be surprised at the depth and variety of content involved in these syllabuses. They also show the vocational element of studying such subjects – students are already learning how to develop and process ideas, assume roles, and make actual works of art.

ASSESSING CREATIVITY

It follows that the assessment of these and other expressive arts syllabuses taken at the high school level contain elements that might be described as 'authentic'. Throughout their expressive arts courses, students participate in and are marked on their skills and competency relative to recognised and established frameworks within these disciplines, often to the extent that they are working as though they are apprentices for future professions. We discuss authentic assessment in more detail in **Chapters 14 and 15**.

A key aspect of the assessment of the arts is that it is a *continuous* process. This underlines the importance of not only assessing the end result, but of becoming 'more aware of children as learners' and giving them the opportunity to develop while helping them to document this development.[10] As Douglas Boughton, former chief examiner of visual arts for the IB Diploma Programme, puts it: 'the day to day formative judgments made by teachers to assist students' progress towards their learning goals play a central role in any successful art education program'.[11]

Donald Schön, in his theory of 'reflection-in-action', encouraged students, climbing up or down a 'ladder of reflection', to learn through doing, with teachers acting as coaches in a supportive environment. Schön, who based much of his research on the study and practice of architecture in the built environment, said that early on in our learning of an arts discipline we often do not even know what we will have to do:

> The paradox of learning a really new competence is this: that a student cannot at first understand what he needs to learn, can learn it only by educating himself, and can educate himself only by beginning to do what he cannot yet understand.[12]

This continuous process of reflecting and learning through doing has led to many expressive arts courses being assessed through portfolios that show the germination and development of skills and ideas through to a final product. Portfolios might contain sketchbooks, examples of what has influenced the student's work, a written record of discussions, debates, critiques and reflections, and/or evidence of work having been put on public display.[13]

Boughton suggests that:

> good portfolios do more than provide evidence for assessment. They drive curriculum in such a way that creative engagement is more likely. A good portfolio will demand students to demonstrate their interests and show the ways in which they have integrated classroom learning with their lives. A good portfolio will require in-depth and sustained reflection, and will provide a good opportunity to engage interest through the pursuit of thematic content. For a portfolio to have the best chance of becoming a living record of students' creative thinking less assessment is better than more.[14]

Arts educators, including Donna Kay Beattie and Douglas Boughton, emphasise the importance of portfolios being directed by teachers but led by students, with a clear, shared understanding of the assessment criteria. They should show an individual's personal growth rather than in relation to others, as well as permitting creative freedom, and they should clearly show – in an ordered manner – the development of the student's learning in such a way that the assessment criteria for a syllabus can be applied.

In broad terms, students of the expressive arts are usually assessed on their knowledge and understanding of their chosen area of study, as well as how well they demonstrate the skills and techniques expected for the level at which they are studying. Students' work is marked on the record that they have kept of what they are doing, how they have explored and developed ideas, and how they have presented their response to a task or stimulus. Assessment is usually carried out by teachers whose work is moderated by sampling, or sometimes by a visiting examiner.

There is an ongoing debate about the extent to which detailed criteria need to be followed in the initial assessment of a student's creativity.[15] Many experienced arts educators feel able to make a holistic assessment of a student's work; and when they first view an artwork, some take the Gestalt approach that 'the whole is something else than the sum of its parts'.[16] Discrete criteria and a common vocabulary enable trained assessors to express their assessment in words, following robust methodology established by respected assessment organisations, which ensures that an assessment is valid, reliable and fair, as well as meeting standards that are comparable to those used in other disciplines.

ASSESSING PERFORMANCE

The assessment of performance also involves a degree of holistic judgement with reference to specific criteria. The Associated Board of the Royal Schools of Music (ABRSM), which is based in the UK but examines the performances of students worldwide, has stringent mark schemes and quality control mechanisms that look at examiners' track records. The grades awarded in ABRSM exams garner credits for further study in music at a higher education level or as a stage towards being a professional performer, and so are subject to strict standards and testing.

According to Lincoln Abbotts, their executive director for strategic development, the ABRSM uses criteria that are designed for graded music exams but which are also a 'valid way to critique any performance'.[17] The five areas assessed are pitch, time, tone, shape and overall performance. Inevitably, Abbotts admits, there will be a degree of subjectivity in scoring each of the criteria: an experienced examiner will 'know when musicians have got the music inside them'.[18]

Graded practical music exams have traditionally included the testing of technical skills, such as the playing of scales and arpeggios, but it could be said that it is only possible to play at a certain level if you already have the technical skills. Partly for this reason, the ABRSM now offers what it calls 'performance grades' as an alternative. If candidates have the tools and technology, they can record themselves playing solo or in front of an audience and have their performance assessed remotely (or they can opt to be assessed in front of an examiner at an exam centre). Candidates for performance exams have to devise a programme, and so – again – can be assessed in a more authentic manner relative to their possible future as music professionals. Abbotts describes this kind of assessment as a 'game changer to celebrate progression and performance'.[19] Remotely assessed music performance exams also have the potential to be more accessible and inclusive, regardless of age or location.

Performance in drama is normally assessed in one of two ways. Assessment organisations either externally moderate assessment that is done in school by teachers or employ a team of examiners who assess filmed performances of students remotely and asynchronously.

According to experienced assessors, the role of the teacher and the facilities in which students are working can play a large role in the marks that get awarded against criteria. This can be because of the following:

- *Unconscious bias*: Teachers might be influenced by other things that they know about a student, such as their behaviour (see **Chapter 7**).
- The *quality of advice* given by the teacher: Students need help, for example, in selecting a 'piece' to perform, such as whether it is right for their voice or emotional maturity.
- *Facilities*: Some schools have theatres that meet professional standards, whereas others do not even have a dedicated space.
- *Local culture*: Audiences can respond in different ways or have expectations of a theatrical performance that might be alien to the examiner. For example, in some countries, everyone claps when someone that they know appears on stage, regardless of whether it is 'appropriate' to do so.

FINAL THOUGHTS

Sometimes it is difficult to assess a performance because no clear criteria exist, or it is not part of the tradition of the genre to assess it. Examples might include folk music, brass bands, slam poetry or rap. Such genres might be studied in a less formal way, with progression achieved from experience and mentoring nurtured in a community. Acknowledgement of someone's ability to perform at a certain level may take many years and be hard-won, but without the need for specific criteria or grading.

In our introduction to this chapter, we mentioned that taste plays a role in our perception of the strength and value of a piece of art – be it a painting, film, dance, play or concert. Sometimes an expressive artwork simply moves us or means more because of prior experience of memories that it stirs.

As the staff writer for *Empty Easel*, Dan, says:

The best art has meaning beyond just an image: perhaps it will bring you to tears, make you laugh, or remind you of something you'd almost forgotten. It also stands out in a crowd and dares to be different. Most importantly (in my opinion) good art is understandable, although it may make you think in ways you never expected to.[20]

Some websites dedicated to art criticism, such as *Empty Easel*, provide lists of visual aspects that they believe are 'generally appealing' to people, including:

- repeating shapes, patterns, and symmetry;
- colours, especially those that complement or enhance each other;
- textures – both visual and physical;
- crops and compositions that focus the eye and keep the viewer's attention;
- movement or flow to guide viewers through the artwork;
- correct or appealing proportions of figures and objects;
- presentation and framing.[21]

The University of Wisconsin–Green Bay proposes 'four levels of formal analysis to explain a work of art' that could be extrapolated for other visual or performing arts:

- *Description*: What do you see?
- *Analysis*: How did the artist do it?
- *Interpretation*: Why did the artist create it, and what does it mean?
- *Judgement*: Is it a good artwork?[22]

Agreed criteria have made it possible to assess the expressive arts but it is hard to take emotion out of the equation. Outside the formal assessment of the expressive arts, we sometimes have to accept that someone we know well likes something more than we do – and they may not be able to tell us why.

KEY TAKEAWAYS

- The assessment of the expressive arts can be challenging because of our tastes, cultures and traditions.
- The study of the expressive arts can be seen as an apprenticeship for a profession.
- Criteria have been established for the assessment of a range of expressive arts that are used to establish a common vocabulary and formalise standards.
- Portfolios that provide evidence of continuous learning are regularly used as a method for assessment, particularly in the visual arts.
- Those who are experienced in the teaching and assessment of the expressive arts are often able to form a holistic judgement about an artwork or performance.

PART C

CREATING THE CONDITIONS FOR LEARNER SUCCESS IN ASSESSMENT

12

PREPARING FOR ASSESSMENT

IN THIS CHAPTER, YOU WILL:

- consider the importance of reflecting on how you learn and do things;
- explore why some people may have a greater inclination to improve their ways of working;
- look at how teachers can encourage students to use assessment formatively;
- review some ways in which students can prepare constructively for examinations.

Once we have done them several times, we take many things that we do for granted. When we prepare food, there will be dishes we can make without reference to a recipe. When we ride a bike, we soon remember how to turn the pedals and guide the handlebars. When we drive, steering the wheel and operating the pedals and levers are second nature. What we do not always appreciate, though, is that when we require less conscious effort to perform tasks, we tend to engage our brains less.

In the late 1960s and 1970s, management consultants in the US[1] began to outline theories that they used in training sessions to help companies improve their ways of working. The 'four stages of learning' model, shown in Figure 12.1, continues to be used widely to demonstrate how we may be more or less aware of our competency to perform various tasks.

The first stage (unconscious incompetence) could describe trying something out for the first time without really giving much thought to what we are doing. To return to the example of preparing food, this might mean throwing some items into a pot, heating for a while and hoping it will be edible. Once we have tasted the food, we might realise that we could have done better, so we are 'consciously incompetent'. Unless we give up at this point, we might then seek help, perhaps in the form of classes or – more simply – by following a recipe. If we do well and understand why, we thus become 'consciously competent'. Several attempts into the future, we may now have our 'go-to' dish that we can make and enjoy with little thought – and so are 'unconscious' in our competence.

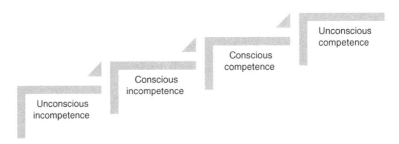

Figure 12.1   Four stages of learning

REFLECTION

You may like to pause for a moment and consider at which stage of learning you are in the things that you do (e.g. playing a musical instrument, photography, gardening, driving).

Let us look in more detail at the example of driving. Some organisations, such as IAM RoadSmart,[2] a road safety charity, take unconscious competence very seriously, especially with reference to car and motorcycle accidents. They run observation courses to improve poor habits, using a 'five-part driving system' and the mnemonic IPSGA to help drivers along their stages of learning:

Information: Absorb information, process it, and give information to others.

Position: Position your vehicle correctly on the road.

Speed: Use your brakes and acceleration to adjust your speed accordingly.

Gear: Select the appropriate gear once you are travelling at the correct speed.

Accelerate: When you are on a straight course after passing any hazards that you have identified, accelerate to an appropriate speed.

If you drive, when was the last time you consciously thought about how well you are driving, or asked someone to observe you? You may remember that in **Chapter 4**, we mentioned the use of checklists to help unconsciously competent people to reduce errors in their work when detecting biases in item design.

In this chapter, we are going to consider how we can evaluate our own levels of competence and readiness to take an assessment, as well as what we can do to create the best conditions for success in our studies, preparations, and the assessment itself. We will look at how teachers can promote positive attitudes to and environments for learning, approaches to learning such as metacognition and self-regulation, and revision and exam techniques.

MINDSET AND ITS INFLUENCE ON LEARNING SUCCESS

In **Chapter 13**, we will look in more detail at assessment from the perspective of mental health and well-being. Some of what we discuss there and in this chapter is underpinned by the concept of 'mindset', outlined by Carol Dweck[3] in her work on social and personality development. Although some other researchers have suggested that the results of her studies are not always replicable,[4] the ideas underpinning 'mindset' remain influential, and the psychology related to it has been picked up by many other authors and commentators.

Matthew Syed has discussed mindset in his books for adults and for children. In *You Are Awesome*,[5] he summarises the attitudes shown by those with fixed and open mindsets, as shown in Table 12.1.

Table 12.1   Fixed and open mindsets

	Fixed mindset	**Open mindset**
Ability	Predetermined from birth.	Can be developed and changed with purposeful practice.
Effort	What's the point? I can't change my abilities.	Have a go. Putting effort in is the only way to get better.
Mistakes	I don't admit them. I don't ask for help.	Mistakes happen. Learn from them and from others.
Feedback	I don't need it. Uncomfortable. I usually ignore it.	Appreciate it. I can't improve unless I know where I'm going wrong.
Challenges	I don't like them. I don't want to look stupid if I get something wrong.	Welcome them. I learn new things by trying – more than once if need be.
Other people's successes	I'm jealous of others. I'm defensive as I assume that I'm not as good as them.	I always try to find out how others achieved their goals so that I can learn from them.

Syed wants to encourage his young readers to reflect on what they do and how they do it so that they can test out new methods or have more than one way of doing something. He asserts that the strongest foundation for this is a belief in yourself, as well as a willingness to listen to advice. Having an open mindset means being prepared to act and take responsibility for your actions.

TEACHERS AS ACTIVATORS OF LEARNING

Certain approaches to teaching and learning have been identified that can promote greater awareness, engagement and responsibility in students. Evidence Based Education's *Great Teaching Toolkit Evidence Review* outlines four priorities for teachers who want to help their students learn more:

1. Understand the content that teachers are teaching and how it is learned.
2. Create a supportive environment for learning.
3. Manage the classroom to maximise the opportunity to learn.
4. Present content, activities and interactions that activate students' thinking.[6]

They divide the fourth dimension, which looks specifically at the learning interface between the teacher and the student, into six 'elements':

- *Structuring*: Giving students an appropriate sequence of learning tasks; signalling learning objectives, rationale, overview, key ideas and stages of progress; matching tasks to learners' needs and readiness; scaffolding and supporting to make tasks accessible to all, but gradually removed so that all students succeed at the required level.
- *Explaining*: Presenting and communicating new ideas clearly, with concise, appropriate, engaging explanations; connecting new ideas to what has previously been learned (and reactivating/checking that prior knowledge); using examples (and non-examples) appropriately to help learners understand and build connections; modelling/demonstrating new skills or procedures with appropriate scaffolding and challenge; using worked/part-worked examples.
- *Questioning*: Using questions and dialogue to promote elaboration and connected, flexible thinking among learners (e.g. 'Why?', 'Compare', etc.); using questions to elicit student thinking; getting responses from all students; using high-quality assessment to evidence learning; interpreting, communicating and responding to assessment evidence appropriately.
- *Interacting*: Responding appropriately to feedback from students about their thinking/knowledge/understanding; giving students actionable feedback to guide their learning.
- *Embedding*: Giving students tasks that embed and reinforce learning; requiring them to practise until learning is fluent and secure; ensuring that once learned, material is reviewed/revisited to prevent forgetting.
- *Activating*: Helping students to plan, regulate and monitor their own learning; progressing appropriately from structured to more independent learning as students develop knowledge and expertise.

The report authors describe this fourth dimension as being central to great teaching, while accepting that it is challenging to know what works because 'student learning is invisible, slow and nonlinear'.[7] Establishing the degree of success of a period of learning – in other words, making learning 'visible' – is one of the main goals of assessment for learning.

ASSESSMENT FOR LEARNING

If we want to gauge how well a student is performing or knows something, it is too late in terms of teaching and learning to wait until a summative assessment (unless it is being used formatively). Students need evidence and feedback from their teachers to understand where they are *now* in relation to what they want to achieve. Teachers and students can then work together to set targets to 'close the gap'. This approach is commonly known as 'assessment for learning'. The approach was first described by Paul Black and Dylan Wiliam.[8]

Assessment for learning is part of a broader movement to involve students more actively in their learning. Jo Boaler, in her book *The Elephant in the Classroom*, aimed at changing children's attitudes about learning mathematics, says that:

> A4L [assessment for learning] is based upon the principle that students should have a full and clear sense of what they are learning, of where they are in the path towards mastery, and what they have to do to become successful.[9]

With clear goals, students can start to 'think like a teacher' and take greater responsibility for their learning.[10]

The three main steps in assessment for learning are:

1. *Questioning* to enable a student, with the help of their teacher, to find out their level.
2. *Feedback* to the student from the teacher about how to improve their learning.
3. An understanding by the student of what *success* looks like for each task that they are doing.

These steps form a continuous loop as students construct their understanding or competencies.

Assessment for learning is closely associated with formative assessment, with the sense of 'shaping' student learning. Cambridge Assessment International Education, in their *Getting Started with Assessment for Learning* resource,[11] make a comparison of formative and summative assessment, as well as illustrating the distinction between what is formal and what is informal (see Table 12.2).

Table 12.2   A comparison of formative and summative assessment

	Formative assessment	**Summative assessment**
Informal	Questioning	Essays in uncontrolled conditions
	Feedback	Portfolios
	Peer assessment	Coursework
	Self-assessment	Teacher assessment
Formal	Further analysis, or tests, exams, essays	Tests
		Exams
	Target-setting	Essays in controlled conditions

A big factor in the assessment for learning approach is that it helps students to look beyond their grades and take notice of the comments which are written by the teacher to guide them on pieces of work that they have done.[12] Some teachers withhold grades until students have read, understood and acted on the comments, or until they have had another go, taking into account the feedback. Feedback should be *task*-focused rather than *ego*-focused, praising some aspects of work and targeting improvement in others, instead of simply saying that someone has done well. The students thus have a richer experience of teaching and learning towards an eventual summative assessment.

As stated in the second dimension described in the *Great Teaching Toolkit*, the environment must be such that teachers and students feel comfortable to take a more honest and collaborative approach to teaching, learning and assessment. The same principles apply to self-assessment and peer assessment, which we will outline next under the umbrella of assessment *as* learning.

ASSESSMENT AS LEARNING

Teachers cannot do the learning for the students – it is up to the students to internalise the process and work out how to move up to the next level.[13] The role of the teacher is crucial in this, not only with regard to constructive feedback, but also in the development and practice of the required skills. This is important because, as Nick Luxmoore says with regard to a student being asked to reflect on his behaviour, 'he can't reflect on himself because no one has ever reflected with him'.[14] Students need to know how to describe how they are learning and to be honest in their self-assessment. This is also true if they are asked to assess their peers so that they can support and learn from them.

Assessment as learning, which can also include the concepts of metacognition and self-regulation (discussed separately below), places more power in the hands of students, moving responsibility and decision-making from the teacher. Figure 12.2, which is a simplified version of a visualisation by the Irish National Forum for the Enhancement of Teaching and Learning in Higher Education,[15] illustrates the overlap between the three types of assessment.

Black and Wiliam[16] described self-assessment as being an essential component of formative assessment. In self-assessment, a learner evaluates their own work and thinks about their own learning. A key point of the self-assessment approach is that it does not make the teacher redundant. The role of the teacher is central to the success of the approach because they establish a suitable environment and the 'rules' for what needs to be done.

The rules include defining success criteria in collaboration with students (but with the end goal of a summative assessment and its criteria in mind), as well as co-designing a framework, plan and timeline. Teachers might encourage students to use graphic organisers such as Gantt charts to organise their work, as well as using methods such as specific, measurable, attainable, relevant and time-bound (SMART) targets to set clear objectives that are achievable and appropriately resourced.

Teachers using peer assessment as part of assessment as learning should naturally ensure that it is done under suitable conditions. The classroom climate needs to be such that students feel able to take risks, as well as being comfortable to give and receive feedback

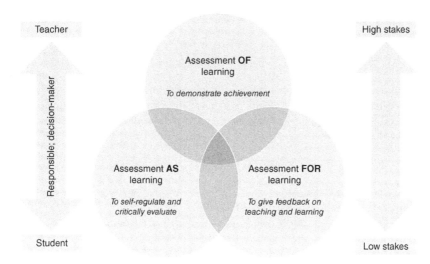

Figure 12.2   Assessment feedback and terminology

between each other. It requires careful preparation and – again – a shared understanding of criteria. Some common strategies to use include:

- *What Works Well (WWW) and Could Be Better (CBB)*: Students tell each other what they think in a way that is designed to keep the tone positive and constructive.
- *Traffic lights*: Students use coloured pens or stickers to mark where a piece of work is meeting the success criteria, not quite there yet, or not meeting them at all.
- *Thermometers*: Students help each other to see where they are closer to meeting criteria (warmer) and when they are further away (cooler) – and so how to 'raise the temperature'.

Both self-assessment and peer assessment help students to hone skills in critical and analytical thinking, as well as communicating their thoughts clearly and constructively to others. Students become more in tune with what is expected of them in an assessment – and obtain practice both in good habits for learning and for working out what to do when they encounter a new but familiar task. You may wish to consider this in relation to the assessment of 21st-century skills that we outlined in **Chapters 9 and 10**.

METACOGNITION AND SELF-REGULATION

Metacognition 'describes the processes involved when learners plan, monitor and evaluate and make changes to their own learning behaviours'.[17] It gives students a broader perspective on their learning beyond a focus on assessment, as well as supporting them in thinking more deeply about what they know and how they are working. It is closely related to the concept of self-regulation, where individuals take a proactive and reflective approach to learning without relying on others.[18]

The Education Endowment Foundation (EEF), in its *Metacognition and Self-Regulated Learning Guidance Report*, breaks down self-regulated learning into three components:

- *Cognition*: The mental process involved in knowing, understanding and learning.
- *Metacognition*: The ways that learners monitor and purposefully direct their learning.
- *Motivation*: The willingness to engage our metacognitive and cognitive skills and apply them to learning.[19]

The report describes some strategies for each of the three components, including:

- *Cognitive strategies*: Memorisation techniques, making different marks with a brush, using different methods to solve equations in maths.
- *Metacognitive strategies*: Monitoring and controlling our cognition (e.g. checking that our technique was accurate or that we selected the best strategy).
- *Motivational strategies*: Convincing oneself to undertake a tricky revision task now – affecting our current well-being – as a way of improving our future well-being in a test tomorrow.

Teachers can model these strategies when they demonstrate how to do something. This might range from how to perform a scientific experiment, to how to understand data, to how to conjugate a verb. A teacher could talk out loud to describe what they are thinking, what they are doing, and how they are reflecting and evaluating both during and afterwards. With practice, students can learn to do the same, eventually internalising their description of what they are doing and thinking without needing to vocalise it.

REFLECTION

Working metacognitively and in collaboration with others naturally opens up new avenues to explore when approaching a task. Here is a simple mathematics example used by Jo Boaler.[20]

How would you normally solve the multiplication problem 18×5? How many other methods can you think of?

Below are the solutions with workings that Boaler's students offered. Are any of the methods the same as those that you thought of?

In your own subject area, reflect how different people may solve common problems in different ways to you, and how this knowledge could be useful when you teach.

$18 + 2 = 20$	$10 \times 5 = 50$	$15 \times 5 = 75$	18×5
$20 \times 5 = 100$	$8 \times 5 = 40$	$3 \times 5 = 15$	$= 10 \times 9$
$5 \times 2 = 10$	$50 + 40 = 90$	$75 + 15 = 90$	$10 \times 9 = 90$
$100 - 10 = 90$			

David Perkins[21] suggested that there are four levels of metacognitive learner through which students might progress (shown in Table 12.3). Recognition of these levels helps teachers to identify where students are on the continuum so that they can support them appropriately.

Table 12.3 Levels of metacognitive learner[22]

Tacit	Aware	Strategic	Reflective
Students are unaware of their metacognitive knowledge. They do not think about any particular strategies for learning, and merely accept if they know something or not.	Students know about some of the kinds of thinking that they do, such as generating ideas and finding evidence. However, their thinking is not necessarily deliberate or planned.	Students organise their thinking by using problem-solving, grouping and classifying, evidence-seeking and decision-making, and so on. They know and apply the strategies that help them learn.	Students are not only strategic about their thinking, but they also reflect upon their learning while it is happening, considering the success – or not – of any strategies that they are using and then revising them as appropriate.

GETTING READY FOR SUMMATIVE ASSESSMENT

Students preparing for examinations need to reflect on how they learn and the best ways to approach revision. It is useful for them to be sensitive to how human psychology and mind-set influence their performance, as well as the importance of being 'match fit' for the big day. We will look in more detail at the latter in **Chapter 13**.

REVISION

As we get closer to a final assessment, we need to check what we need to know, distil it into manageable chunks, understand how we are going to be assessed, and find opportunities to practise. Here are some tips for what might work in the last few days before an examination:[23]

- Focus on what you know so that you can apply it in question answers (e.g. match facts and figures about a topic to possible questions).
- Know the facts. Spend time quizzing yourself and others about specific facts. One way of doing this with others is to make cards that each have a question and answer on them and find the pairs – students learn more if they make up the quizzes themselves.
- Use past and specimen papers to get a feel for them and know how to read them.
- Interrogate the questions. Pick apart the wording of a question from a previous exam paper, highlight and underline the key words, and think of topics and approaches to answering.[24]

Again, students who have been given the opportunity to monitor and explore how they learn and who have a repertoire of methods at their disposal are more likely to be ready to revise independently and in a measured way. With reference to Table 12.2, well-prepared students should by now be at the strategic and reflective stages of learning.

EXAM TECHNIQUE

The University of Sheffield offers some useful advice on exam technique. It is aimed at university-level students but is pertinent for those taking assessments at any age. Once again, being clear about your objective and having a strategy, tools and techniques in mind helps to create conditions for success. Here are some general tips adapted from the university's website:

- At the beginning of an exam:
  o read the instructions carefully so that you know how many questions you have to answer and how long the exam is;
  o choose the questions you want to answer and which you will do first;
  o allocate an appropriate amount of time to each question, also reserving time for checking at the end (as well as recharging between answers).

- Before you start writing:
  o look for 'action' verbs to understand how you are expected to answer the question – exam syllabuses often provide a list of common words and define them;
  o consider if the question gives you parameters and whether it contains any key words or phrases;
  o focus on the question that is asked – do not just write everything that you know.

- As you write your answer:
  o keep an eye on the clock and stick as closely as possible to the time you have allocated to the question;
  o if a question is divided into sections and you are running out of time, focus on the early parts where you can usually gain some easy marks, using bullet points if need be rather than full sentences.[25]

FINAL THOUGHTS

At the beginning of this chapter, we discussed the four stages of competence: unconscious incompetence, conscious incompetence, conscious competence and unconscious competence. The methods we have outlined in assessment *for* learning and assessment *as* learning help students to move from the first level and through the second and third levels. A summative assessment *of* learning is part of the process towards the fourth level – and eventual mastery.

An awareness that we can become unconsciously competent in how we perform, including in our professional lives, should prompt us to check from time to time whether we have picked up any bad habits and might need to slip back a level to recalibrate. Some people have also argued for a fifth level of competence, which could involve teaching or training others – mentoring or coaching them on the methods they might use to assess themselves and improve how they work.

There are always better and other ways to do things than those to which we have become habituated. As educators, we can pass this philosophy on to others, as well as encouraging them to keep learning and preparing, particularly when the end goal is an important examination.

KEY TAKEAWAYS

- We all have progressive levels of awareness about how well we perform particular tasks.
- Whether we think we can improve depends on our mindset and willingness to act.
- Teachers who establish a positive environment with meaningful dialogue can help students to learn more about how they learn and encourage them to explore new methods.
- Students can become more independent and responsible in their learning, using approaches such as metacognition and self-regulation.
- As we prepare for and take assessments, we can benefit from careful preparation and practice.

13

ASSESSMENT, MENTAL HEALTH AND WELL-BEING

IN THIS CHAPTER, YOU WILL:

- learn more about what affects our mental health and well-being;
- be able to recognise and identify the signs and causes of test anxiety;
- learn some ways of helping students to be more positive about how they feel and how they can function.

Many people speak in broad terms about mental health. We all have mental health, just as we all have physical health, but we usually find it easier to talk about the latter because it is easier to see and describe. How we feel mentally is often hidden and experienced internally; but thanks to information campaigns and the increasing removal of the stigma surrounding mental health, we are now more able to talk about how we feel and seek support.

The World Health Organization (WHO) says that mental health relates to how – and to what extent – we can realise our abilities, actualise our intellectual and emotional potential, cope with the normal stresses of life, be productive, and contribute to our community.[1] The state of our mental health can sometimes be good and sometimes less so, depending on our interactions with others and the tasks that we are doing.

How well we feel (our 'well-being') relates to how happy, healthy or in control we think we are – not just at one particular time, but in general. Current academic research treats well-being from two perspectives: 'hedonic', which defines well-being in terms of pain avoidance and pleasure attainment and focuses on happiness; and 'eudaemonic', which defines well-being in terms of the degree to which a person is 'fully functioning' and focuses on approaches to self-realisation.[2] The extent of an individual's well-being can be understood as symptomatic of their mental health.

Gordon Harold, professor of the psychology of education and mental health at the University of Cambridge, has demonstrated through longitudinal studies that children's mental health is not specifically related to genetics. He states that it is the promotion of positive home and school environments that 'substantially affects children's long-term outcomes'. In other words, 'all parents and carers, as well as teachers and other professionals can make a significant difference to children's life chances', supporting them to have healthy minds.[3]

Stress can be a challenge or a threat that is taken positively or negatively. In general terms, stress is a 'response occurring when one feels what can be achieved is less than what is expected or desired'.[4] If we perceive what is making us feel stressed as a *challenge*, as well as focusing on success and having positive self-belief, the result can be motivation, harder work and better performance. If, however, we perceive a stressor as a *threat*, it can cause anxiety. This can disrupt us cognitively, and as a result reduce performance. In short, *stress* can be positive or negative; *anxiety* is only negative.

In this chapter, we are going to explore how different approaches to mental health and well-being can both help and hinder students when they are preparing for assessments. We will discuss test anxiety, as well as its origins and its impact, and we will look at the types of routines and interventions that can be put in place before, during and after the times when we are being assessed.

WHAT ARE THE SIGNS OF TEST ANXIETY?

Most of us experience anxiety in our lives and to some degree when we are being assessed on our performance, but high anxiety is when we experience symptoms *most* of the time in assessment situations. Individuals lie on a continuum and suffer from test anxiety to varying degrees.

REFLECTION

What do you experience when you are anxious in an assessment or other situation? How are you affected cognitively, emotionally and physically? Does it make you 'fight', 'take flight' or 'freeze'?

Ofqual, working with Liverpool John Moores University, describe three main ways in which high test anxiety manifests:

- *Cognitive* (related to thoughts), such as:
  - going blank in an exam;
  - having difficulty concentrating;
  - having negative thoughts about past performance or the consequences of failure.

- *Affective* (related to emotions), including:
  - feeling excessive tension;
  - feeling panic;
  - feeling overwhelmed;
  - not feeling in control.

- *Physical*, including:
  - feeling dizzy or faint;
  - sweating;
  - experiencing a fast heartbeat or a tight, churning stomach;
  - feeling that you have jelly or wobbly legs.[5]

It is estimated that only a small number of students per class are likely to suffer from test anxiety – and it is more common in females than in males. It is suggested that boys traditionally worry less because – in general – they prepare less, ask less for support, downplay the importance of exams and seek other distractions. Anxiety among both boys and girls does increase, however, as assessments become more important for future life chances.[6]

Some commentators maintain that 'a bit of stress is good for you', but this might not be the case for everyone. Studies so far suggest that high levels of test anxiety are generally associated with small reductions in test performance.[7] The fact that we have been made anxious can, however, be detrimental to our mental health in the longer term. And whatever your perception of the impact of stress on performance or well-being, it is in everyone's interests to make candidates feel as comfortable as possible when taking assessments.

WHAT ARE THE CAUSES OF TEST ANXIETY?

According to Ofqual, test anxiety is usually as a result of one or more of the following factors:

- *Intro-personal*: An individual will have their own beliefs about their academic ability, why they want to succeed, and the ways in which they cope.
- *Interpersonal*: The ways in which a student interacts with their teachers, parents and peers can increase or reduce test anxiety.
- *Assessment-specific*: Some types or features of assessments are more likely to induce anxiety than others.[8]

In its review of the literature, Ofqual observed that the first two factors can be summarised under four related themes: academic competence beliefs, coping, motivation, and emotional contagion.[9]

ACADEMIC COMPETENCE BELIEFS

Throughout our lives, we all make evaluations about how competent we are, including with regard to taking assessments. If we feel that we are less able (regardless of our actual ability) and cannot do much about it, we are more likely to be anxious.[10]

COPING

Some students are more capable than others of dealing with the pressure of high-stakes exams. David Putwain and colleagues refer to this as 'academic buoyancy', a trait that can lead to resilience and perhaps greater circumspection about the importance of assessments.[11] There are those who cope with anxiety through avoidance – of revision or of the examination itself. Most candidates will, however, have devised strategies for coping, some of which we will refer to later in the chapter.

MOTIVATION

There are two types of motivation: intrinsic and extrinsic. Some students will be stimulated by a subject, as well as by being assessed on their knowledge, skills and understanding. They may have specific goals for achievement in mind or be in pursuit of mastery.[12] Others may evaluate their performance against their peers or against standards that they cannot attain. Either type of motivation can lead to greater or less anxiety and better or worse results.

EMOTIONAL CONTAGION

Students, particularly in adolescence, will be influenced by others,[13] including how they feel about assessments. Throughout their school life, but particularly when they reach high-stakes exams, a student may receive pressure from their parents and teachers to do well. Parents and teachers often make 'fear appeals', which are intended to motivate academic behaviour.[14] Such fear appeals may be more about a parent's or teacher's own motivations or perceptions than those of the student. According to Merryn Hutchings, around 70 per cent of teachers indicate that their stress levels can affect how they interact with students.[15] A student who is the recipient of a fear appeal can become more anxious, resulting in negative consequences. Emotional contagion can alternatively be positive if a parent or teacher enthuses about a subject and passes this on.

Some types of assessment can induce more anxiety than others. Research suggests, for example, that candidates generally feel more comfortable with multiple-choice questions than with those that require longer answers. Usually, what we do in a high-stakes assessment will not be different to what we have already practised, but it is the purpose of the assessment (e.g. for a qualifying grade as a basis for entry to a later educational phase or employment) that can make it more fearful. If those who are designing the assessment of a construct can show that it could be assessed in a way that provokes less anxiety – and that this does not interfere with the assessment of the construct – they may choose to change it.[16]

Candidates are more likely to experience anxiety in assessments that are more 'social' in nature, such as those in front of an audience of one or more people. Oral exams are seen by many as stressful, although some might thrive when given the opportunity to speak rather than write. Indeed, in some assessments, such as of theatre arts or music, having an audience is considered a necessary and legitimate part of measuring a performance.

As we will see in **Chapter 14**, some students may prefer assessment that is continuous or modular or which takes place in an authentic environment. Such assessments can, of course, also lead to greater or lesser degrees of anxiety. Some students may feel the pressure of deadlines, especially if they have several in a short time period or the deadlines conflict with other activities on the course they are studying. Some may benefit from teacher reminders about what needs to be done; others may feel the opposite. There is mixed evidence about whether linear or modular exams induce greater anxiety.[17]

HOW CAN WE MANAGE TEST ANXIETY?

Some individuals suffer from poor mental health that requires professional diagnosis and support, such as dedicated counselling. It is important to know this and to have appropriate referral systems in place. Most students, regardless of whether they experience test anxiety, will, however, benefit from some of the interventions below that have been suggested by experts. We already saw in **Chapter 12** how we can support students through metacognition and self-regulation to find alternative ways of approaching a piece of academic work. Our focus here is above all on sit-down examinations, but the ideas can be applied across all forms of assessment.

REFLECTION

Before reading on, reflect on how you manage stress ahead of a situation that might provoke anxiety. What tools and techniques do you use? What have you learned from others or seen others do? If you are a teacher, what could you do that would make exam preparation less worrisome for students?

PREPARATION

If you have an important event taking place at a fixed time in the future, you need to be ready for it. It is no surprise that the mottos of several organisations refer to this, such as 'Be Prepared' (Scouts and Guides) or '*Semper paratus*' (United States Coast Guard). Benjamin Franklin wrote that 'by failing to prepare, you are preparing to fail', and some military establishments quote the 6Ps: 'prior planning and preparation prevent poor performance'.

Preparation for high-stakes exams takes place over a period of time in schools. Teachers follow a syllabus as a guide for what students need to learn – and should normally have reviewed examples of previous assessments. Teachers usually introduce students to the scope of the course that is set out in the syllabus, as well as its objectives and the means by which they will be assessed. When students are ready, their teacher will show them what the final examination(s) will look like and give them an opportunity to practise, usually in a controlled environment (e.g. taking a mock examination).

The best environment for preparation is a positive one. This means encouraging healthy, cooperative relationships between students, as well as between students and the teacher; designing lessons that are rich in opportunities; focusing and building on strengths and abilities; and giving meaningful feedback. It also means being aware, as a teacher, when you are tempted to make a fear appeal – support and nurture are better than coercion.

ROUTINES

Successful sportspeople create routines to help them focus and avoid distractions or having to think about things that are peripheral to their goal. Sometimes routines can become obsessional or too rigid, so it is important to allow flexibility and to make routines as natural as possible. Chris McLeod, a researcher in sport and exercise nutrition at Loughborough University, suggests that both sports stars and students should 'train as [they] would want to perform on the day' – you should have confidence that the routine you have created will provide you with what you need.[18] And if you are worried that you might forget to take something with you on the day of an examination, apply what is known as a 'Gibsonian affordance': place what you need somewhere that you will see it before you set out for the exam (e.g. by the door). Pack and check your bag the night before so that you have less to remember in the morning.

FITNESS

A general level of fitness is advisable, particularly if you are going to be taking a series of assessments. McLeod underlines the importance of preparation in the longer term, and not to change something just before you take an exam that could disturb your equilibrium or make you overtired. On the day of an assessment, you should do nothing different to your usual routine. For example, if time permits and you would normally walk or run first thing in the morning, do it; otherwise, do not.

As far as possible, you should get into the habit of how you will sit in an exam. The ideal posture is to sit up straight, with your feet flat on the floor, and hard chairs in exam halls usually allow little other option. You should also get used to writing with a pen for an extended period of time. It may be useful to strengthen your muscles with a handgrip or simply by practising writing texts of increasing length.

Physical activity is also important for your mental health. It is well known that taking exercise can help to combat stress and reduce anxiety at all ages. If you are monitoring how far you have gone or how fast you have completed a particular activity, you should see progress over time, which can be motivating. We secrete endorphins when we exercise – one of the four hormones known to make us happy.

And we must not forget the role that sleep has to play in our fitness. Matthew Walker, in his book *Why We Sleep*, explains how our brain's hippocampus has limited capacity for storage, and so we need a means by which we can move memories and information to other parts of our brain. His research shows that sleep restores our capacity for learning, making more secure that which has been learned the day before.[19]

NUTRITION

McLeod recommends again that you should not make radical changes to the ways you eat or drink on the day of an exam. There are, however, foodstuffs and drinks that are better for you than others. Sugar, for example, gives you a 'quick fix', and so can be good in the middle of a long exam, but should be limited to help you maintain concentration, sustain energy and provide stability over a period of time. It is better not to become dependent on caffeine. Caffeine is good for concentration and alertness, and can keep you going for longer, but it can increase anxiety, including giving you 'the shakes', for which you might overcompensate by consuming more coffee or sugar.

Water should also be drunk in moderation: it is possible to have too much as it can dilute some micronutrients in your blood, which is bad for your blood pressure and concentration. It is, however, beneficial to be hydrated to perform at your best. McLeod recommends that you should drink when you feel thirsty and not have a prescribed daily amount in mind. The exception to this is in humid climates where you may not realise that you are becoming dehydrated as you are sweating. It probably goes without saying that it is not a good idea to drink alcohol before taking an exam. It is a depressant, and – as a toxic substance – can be harder for your body to process, using up vital energy.

Overall, McLeod recommends what he calls 'stability meals' so that you have no need for quick hits. If we can, we should all eat lean protein first and foremost, supplemented by vegetables and legumes and a small number of starchy, fibrous foods. Natural, locally sourced, unprocessed foods are best to make you the fittest – both physically and mentally – for anxiety-provoking situations.

SUPPORT

Coaching, mentoring and courses on techniques such as cognitive behavioural therapy (CBT) or mindfulness-based stress reduction (MBSR) are increasingly common in educational environments.

These give students an opportunity for self-reflection, talking through their emotions, and finding alternative ways of thinking, doing and being.

The coaching and mentoring we are talking about here is the modern, facilitative approach that helps to change mindsets. Coaching done properly enables the person being coached to talk through individual challenges and – with gentle prompting from a qualified coach – verbalise both how they feel mentally and what they can do to change the situation. John Whitmore popularised a model to follow in coaching, using the mnemonic 'GROW':

- *Goal*: Where do you want to get to?
- *Reality*: Where are you now?
- *Options*: How might you make progress?
- *Way forward*: What actions can you take to reach your goal?[20]

GROW helps us to make sense – in a positive way – of what we need to do to influence how we act. It gives us a framework for thinking through and working towards what we want to achieve.

Amy Burke and Kevin Hawkins, who deliver workshops and write about mindfulness, suggest a 'backward design approach' when thinking about preparation for key events such as assessments. If the target is an assessment, how should we approach it?[21] Students need to be ready for that moment when they open an exam paper. Some may feel excitement, while others may feel panic. Either way, this may lead to a candidate misreading a question or needing to take precious time to be in the right state of mind to begin writing their answers.

Burke and Hawkins suggest that students should get to know their bodies, or they can 'get tripped up by their own physiology'.[22] We should all become cognisant of and feel comfortable with different sensations in our bodies. Mindfulness focuses on being more present and also on 'acceptance'. We should be less critical of ourselves, and simply notice thoughts, feelings and emotions so that we can attend to them and alleviate anxiety using techniques that we have practised.

Such techniques include breathing exercises, which can be used before and during an exam to 'centre' or 'reboot' ourselves. Breathing exercises can be done without anyone else knowing as they are a natural part of our existence and something personal. One easy exercise that Burke and Hawkins suggest is what they call 'Plus 2': breathe in and out and count in seconds at the same time to find your own rhythm, then add two seconds each time you exhale. Alternatively, imagine you are holding a cup of hot chocolate – inhale as you 'smell' it and exhale as you 'blow' on it. When we think about how we breathe, we are helping to 'anchor' ourselves and intentionally engaging our parasympathetic nervous system so that we can take greater control of our emotions.

TIPS FROM STUDENTS

The BBC invited some students to share their experiences with other exam-takers.[23] The students emphasised the importance of maintaining a healthy work-life balance, including a social life and regular exercise. They also stressed how important it is to open up and talk with parents, friends and teachers, as well as having and agreeing upon appropriate expectations. Once an exam is over, their recommendation was to stay calm, refocus and get ready for the next one. Burke and Hawkins recommend students giving themselves a treat, and – when they are ready – reflecting on their own or with others on the experience.

The students also talked about how to be in the best shape mentally on results day. If you have not achieved the results that you wanted, they suggest giving yourself time to process the news before analysing what went wrong – and why. Talk to people and seek the advice of experts on next steps. In the students' opinion, you have only made a mistake if you do not learn from it. Exams can be the culmination of years of study and hard work, but there are always options – and these may lead to a better opportunity. As one of the students said, 'Exams don't define who you are'.[24]

FINAL THOUGHTS

If we want to be successful, we also need to identify and understand what might get in the way. In the 1970s, Tim Gallwey, the former tennis star turned coach, formulated this idea in a simple equation:

performance = potential *minus* interference[25]

In the right environment, with appropriate support, and with a clear plan in mind to improve our methods and overcome barriers, we can create the conditions for success in what we are doing. Success can be bred from how we look after our body and mind.

KEY TAKEAWAYS

- We all have mental health, which can be good or bad according to our personality traits and the situations in which we find ourselves.
- Stress can be positive or negative, leading to a better or reduced performance.
- Test anxiety can result from intro-personal, interpersonal and assessment-specific factors.
- We can help to alleviate test anxiety through preparation, routines, fitness, nutrition and support.
- It can be beneficial to reflect on and put into words how we feel when we are anxious, as well as using facilitative coaching techniques to learn, improve and accept how we feel.

14

ASSESSMENT FOR ALL

IN THIS CHAPTER, YOU WILL:

- learn about the challenges that some students may face when taking assessments;
- learn what assessment organisations do to enable students to access more traditional forms of assessment;
- explore some alternative assessment methodologies, such as designing assessments with inclusivity in mind.

Outside, the students are waiting – some chatting cheerily in groups, some desperately reviewing their notes, some closing their eyes to visualise diagrams or equations, some checking stationery or water bottles, some pacing in circles. The doors open and a pair of stern-faced invigilators admit those waiting in an orderly manner. The rules and regulations have been checked, and the exam hall is ready.

Most students quickly find their allotted row and desk, while others need directions to where they will be seated. Some students' desks are larger and sometimes their chairs are different. They have their own clock and their own signs to indicate the length of time that they will be at their desks. These students are in the area of the room furthest from the exit so that the other students in the regular rows – who will finish their exam sooner – will not disturb them as they leave at the end of the normal allocated time.

This scenario – or variations of it – plays out all over the world many times per year. It paints a picture of exam-takers, each with their own story, each with their individual needs and ways of managing them, and of a small group that is singled out to be given extra time or space. Elsewhere, perhaps in a building nearby, other students from the same cohort will sit in their own room, supported more closely by an adult or by technology, sometimes with the freedom to walk around and take breaks.

In this chapter, we are going to consider the challenges that some students may encounter in assessment from the perspective of special educational needs and neurodiversity. We are going to look at how assessment organisations aim to make assessments equitable and how teaching institutions can best prepare students for high-stakes assessments. We will also explore how some education organisations are making assessments more inclusive, as well as considering how the redesign of assessments may be beneficial for all.

SPECIAL EDUCATIONAL NEEDS AND NEURODIVERSITY

'Special educational needs' refers to learners who have significantly greater difficulty learning and accessing assessments than the majority of other learners of the same age. It also refers to learners who need support and adjustments to overcome long-term barriers (such as sensory impairments or health conditions) when learning and accessing assessments.

The word 'neurodiversity' recognises that our brains ('neuro-') naturally vary from person to person (i.e. they are 'diverse'), and that this is part of human variation. For some, it is an emotive word, pitching those who are considered 'neurotypical' against those who are considered 'neurodivergent', but we intend it here in an inclusive sense, celebrating that we all see and perceive the world in our own way – and some of us may interact with the world and its practices more differently than others.

Harvey Blume, writing in *The Atlantic* in 1998 with particular reference to the high-tech revolution, suggested that 'neurodiversity may be every bit as crucial for the human race as biodiversity is for life in general. Who can say what form of wiring will prove best at any given moment?'[1] Nearly two decades later, as the concept became more widely accepted, Nobuo Masataka underlined that 'understanding learning differences as neurodiversity can represent a paradigm shift in the way that we think about learning in the classroom, and has the power to transform the way we teach'.[2] If we take neurodiversity into account in our practices, we can make education more accessible for everyone, including those who – at least on the surface – are getting along fine.

It might also transform the way that we assess. As we have discussed, assessment is inseparable from teaching and learning. UNESCO's *Global Education Monitoring Report* states that 'an inclusive learning experience requires inclusive curriculum, textbooks and assessment practices – the links between them are often ignored, with one being changed while others are not'.[3] The latter tends to lag behind, not accommodating different needs – and often to the exclusion of learners – frequently because it is driven by external factors such as accountability measures. Sometimes it is assumed to be enough if 'easy' adjustments are made, such as giving extra time to exam candidates. Making assessments more inclusive to accommodate diverse needs runs deeper than that.

WHAT CHALLENGES DO SOME STUDENTS FACE?

It is important to remember that not only students with special educational needs, or who might be termed as or identify as being 'neurodiverse', face barriers to learning and assessment.

We all experience challenges that are visible or hidden which we may have overcome or learned to live with. Some people may experience more than one barrier, and it may be a combination of these – rather than one barrier on its own – that presents a challenge for assessment.

Table 14.1 sets out a selection of eight common challenges that we may meet.

Table 14.1   A selection of neurodiverse challenges[4]

Behavioural	Concentration and attention	Communication and language	Executive functions
Regulating and conveying emotions (in)appropriately (e.g. frustration, disengagement, withdrawal, anger)	Impulsivity, distractibility, hyper-focus, information overload	Speaking, listening and the social use of language	Time management, planning, prioritising organisation, working memory
Motor	**Mental health**	**Literacy**	**Numeracy**
Fine motor, gross motor and balance difficulties, including dyspraxia	Depression, anxiety, eating disorders, obsessive-compulsive disorder (OCD)	Reading, spelling or writing content, including dyslexia	Difficulties with mathematics competency, including dyscalculia

REFLECTION

Before proceeding further with your reading, reflect on each of the eight challenges above and consider: (a) whether you or people you know have experienced them; and, if so, (b) how the challenges have affected your or their approaches to learning and assessment.

Clearly, assessment cannot be inclusive unless it takes special needs and neurodiversity into account, but to what extent is this currently the case in standardised testing?

ACCESS ARRANGEMENTS FOR HIGH-STAKES ASSESSMENTS

England's qualifications and examinations regulator Ofqual describes the different types of arrangements and adjustments that may be available to students (described here as 'candidates'):

- Access arrangements are the provisions made for candidates, agreed before they take an assessment, to ensure that they can be *validly assessed* and are *not unfairly disadvantaged* due to a disability, temporary illness or injury.

- Access arrangements for candidates experiencing a temporary illness or injury, or some other event outside of the learner's control, are known as *special consideration*.
- Access arrangements should not be confused with post-examination *adjustments* to the marks of candidates who have not been able to demonstrate their ability in an assessment due to exceptional circumstances, such as bereavement, at the time of assessment.[5]

Access arrangements are also known as 'accommodations' (particularly in the US) and 'alternative arrangements' (particularly in Australia).

Ofqual's 2019 report showed that in the previous year, 90 per cent of the 5,420 exam centres in England had approved access arrangements for one or more of their students, with the most common type being 25 per cent extra time (for 20 per cent of students). It may be of interest to note that the report showed in secondary, non-selective, non-independent schools, 17 per cent of students had 25 per cent extra time; in independent schools, 26 per cent of students had 25 per cent extra time; and in post-16 education, 23 per cent of students had 25 per cent extra time.

Some people have questioned the efficacy of giving students extra time – and whether all that have been granted it really need it.[6] Research is light on the advantage that extra time gives. For some students, it adds to their discomfort of being in an assessment environment and can mean an accumulation of many additional hours over the course of a series of examinations in a short period of time. Others have questioned whether access arrangements are fairly available, including whether those with financial or other advantages may be more likely to obtain them.[7]

Assessment organisations require that requests for access arrangements be made based on evidence of the student's barrier to assessment and evidence of the student's need. In their rules, they set out detailed clauses describing the provision and practice of each type of arrangement. The volume of students and the percentage needing access arrangements means that assessment organisations often have to trust that those making requests are doing so for honest and genuine reasons. Requests are regulated by sampling alongside other checks that are made to see if accredited assessment centres are operating according to the rules to which they have agreed.

Schools can also make requests for modified papers, which 'are prepared for candidates with, for example, a range of visual impairments and/or significant language comprehension disorders in order to allow them to demonstrate their skills, knowledge and understanding'.[8]

Table 14.2 shows the types of access arrangements or modified question papers that can be requested for students presenting for examinations.

If students are going to benefit as much as intended from access arrangements, they need support to do so. Teachers should discuss with students how best, for example, to use their extra 25 per cent time; how to make the most of their supervised rest breaks, both physically and mentally; and/or how technical and other aids can help them. If students are to work with an amanuensis (someone who takes dictation) or have another person assisting them in an assessment, they will need to practise and agree on such matters as spelling, punctuation and – especially in a timed examination setting – the speed of dictation.[10]

As we have discussed in previous chapters, assessment organisations seek to provide assessments that are as fair as possible to students. The Cambridge Assessment *Code of*

Table 14.2   Types of access arrangements or modified question papers[9]

Colour-naming	Coloured overlays	Computer reader	Exemptions	Less than 25 per cent extra time
More than 25 per cent extra time	Human reader	Practical assistant	Prompter	Reading aloud (candidate)
Reading pens	Scribe	Supervised rest breaks	Transcript of candidate's work	Visual aids
Voice-activated software	Word processor	Braille	Coloured paper	A4 18-point bold
18-point bold enlarged to A3	A3 unmodified	Simplified carrier language	Tactile diagrams	Live speaker (listening CDs)

Practice states that 'question papers and mark schemes will minimise construct-irrelevance variance'.[11] And one of the commitments to this aim states that:

> Question papers will be such that the effect on the results of the test of irrelevant factors (e.g. gender, language, socio-economic group) is minimised and cultural bias is avoided (unless the perception of such bias is itself what is being assessed).[12]

This extends to situations where students are not taking exams in their first or strongest language. Research by Cambridge Assessment International Education suggested that an ability to use English at level B2 of the Common European Framework of Reference for Languages (CEFR) was 'useful' to access non-language IGCSE assessments and that level C1 gave an 'added advantage' for humanities subjects.[13] Further research proposes that another language scale be created to take into account the greater demands of using academic as opposed to social language in assessments.[14]

You may remember that in **Chapter 4**, we discussed how item writers work to avoid bias when developing examination papers. They also receive guidance on how best to take students' language needs into consideration when they write assessment items, including the following:

- Ensure that instructions are precise and convey exactly what the student is expected to do.
- Avoid long or structurally complex sentences;
- Avoid phrasal verbs (e.g. 'put up with').
- It is important to preserve the flavour of source texts; however, sensible editing can benefit all students.
- Try to standardise instructional language and command words.
- Use line spacing to separate points and to assist reading.
- Consider visual support.
- Do not test language if it is not part of the assessment.[15]

Assessment organisations are constantly researching ways to disadvantage as few students as possible, with reference to guidance from regulators.

RETHINKING ASSESSMENT TO MAKE IT MORE INCLUSIVE

So far in this chapter, we have looked at to what extent students – regardless of their individual needs – are required to conform to traditional methods of assessment. Access arrangements provide an important mainstream experience for students who otherwise risk being excluded or ranked below their true ability,[16] but are there other routes that could make assessment more inclusive for all students, regardless of their neurodiversity or purposefully taking it into account?

Judith Waterfield and Bob West, in their Staff-Student Partnership for Assessment Change and Evaluation (SPACE) initiative, found three approaches to inclusive assessment in higher education that may also be considered relevant to primary and secondary levels of learning:

- *contingent* (e.g. 'special arrangements' such as extra time, amanuensis, own room, etc.), which essentially describes a form of assimilation into an existing system;
- *alternative* (e.g. a viva voce instead of a written assignment), providing possibilities for a minority of disabled students;
- *inclusive* (e.g. a flexible range of assessment modes made available to all), a method of assessing the same learning outcomes in different ways.[17]

The former is what usually happens in practice, but the report authors' preference is for the latter, and they ask 'how assessment of learning can be made generally applicable, without resorting to compensation, and therefore viable and equitable for the broadest student constituency'.[18]

Universal Design for Learning (UDL), first defined by David Rose, Anne Meyer and colleagues at Harvard University,[19] is an educational framework that promotes flexibility in teaching and learning through providing learners with:

- multiple means of representation (various ways of acquiring information and knowledge);
- multiple means of engagement (to mirror learners' interests, challenge them appropriately and motivate them to learn);
- multiple means of expression (for demonstrating what they know).

UDL is a good starting point for answering Waterfield and West's question, in terms of looking not only at how candidates can express what they know, but also how they learn – and to what extent they are engaged in their learning.

If we consider inclusive education to be proactive rather than reactive, and use the principles of frameworks such as UDL, we can anticipate, plan for and mitigate challenges to learning. This in turn reduces the need for individual access arrangements or adjustments. The intention is to maintain high expectations for all students, not to reduce standards, and to teach and eventually assess their knowledge, understanding and skills in a way that is the fairest.

As we saw in **Chapter 13**, teachers need to help students find strategies for coping with challenging situations, regardless of whether they have recognised neurodiverse needs.

While it is important to reduce or remove barriers, it is also important to help students build resilience by scaffolding their learning and building them up gradually to be ready to take an assessment. We should also be conscious that a sudden alteration in arrangements, such as a changed exam location or an amended start time, can dismantle students' strategies. Some students may, for example, use strategies such as visualising where they will sit or how long before an exam they should eat or drink. Without a strategy, a student's confidence can be adversely affected, leading to cognitive overload, which in turn has a negative impact on exam performance.

Robert Eaton and Abby Osborne at the University of Bath use patterns rather than labels when considering students' neurodiversity.[20] They suggest three 'contexts' – *physical* (where), *cultural* (what) and *cognitive* (how) – that can help us to consider assessment from a student's perspective, as well as how best to prepare and advise them.

For example, for *all* students in the exam hall described at the beginning of this chapter:

- What is the environment like, and might it distract students in any way, such as in terms of sound, lighting or an individual candidate's location in the room? (*physical*)
- How clear are the instructions for and within the exam paper? (*cultural*)
- How has the assessment been designed to enable students to show what they know? (*cognitive*)

REFLECTION

Read again the first two paragraphs of this chapter, picturing a similar situation where you have been a candidate or an invigilator. What physical, cultural and cognitive considerations may have made that assessment experience more inclusive for all candidates? Think about it in terms of both before and during (as well as after) the assessment.

Ideally, by the time that students reach a final examination, they should have had plenty of practice, be clear about what they have to do, and not have to worry about any surprises. Sally Brown, quoted in Plymouth University's *Inclusive Assessment Good Practice Guide*, says that inclusivity can be enhanced by:

- *feed-in* (set up, briefing, preparation and practice, clear assessment and marking criteria, question and answer sessions, discussion);
- *feedback* (written, verbal, grades, after all assessments);
- *feedforward* (formative, through discussion, midway reviews, self-assessment, peer and tutor feedback, to help stage learning and tasks).[21]

These three 'feeds' underline again the extent to which teaching, learning and assessment approaches should be designed together to support students' development towards achieving the learning outcomes of a course or syllabus.

To be as inclusive as possible, all three 'feeds' should at least be guided by the following principles, written for the purposes of feedback:

- Use clear, literal, unambiguous language and concise sentences.
- Electronic feedback should have clear font and text size.
- If feedback is handwritten, make sure it is legible.
- Offer opportunities to give feedback orally, not just in written form, so that students can choose.
- If setting up a meeting to give feedback, make sure that students know what to expect.

The Irish National Forum for the Enhancement of Teaching and Learning in Higher Education echoes this, suggesting that assessment and feedback should be 'manageable', 'foster a partnership' between teachers and students, and 'empower students to become self-regulated learners'.[22]

DIVERSITY IN ASSESSMENT

A number of universities are considering how to make assessment more inclusive. Universities often have greater flexibility in the assessment 'diet' compared to assessments in regulated qualifications for younger students, such as GCSEs, but some of the creative thinking from higher education could help to bring greater diversity to assessment at all levels of education.

Plymouth University guides its staff by *7 Steps to Inclusive Assessment*:

1. Underpin your assessment with good design principles.
2. Use a variety of assessment methods within your module/programme.
3. Incorporate choice into your assessment.
4. Design inclusive exams.
5. Consider how technology could assist.
6. Prepare, engage and support students in the assessment process.
7. Monitor, review and share practice.[23]

The university interviewed some of its students, who broadly agreed that staff adhere to these steps.[24] Some still felt, however, that certain assessors place greater value on final examinations because that is the way they have always done things or because they see purpose in knowing how well students can sit down and concentrate. The students also felt that assessments should be an application of your ability to solve a problem, not a memory test or example of how well you can cope with being in an exam hall and focus for a specific period of time. The students remarked that such 'old-fashioned' approaches to assessment are less relevant to the skills required to perform in 'modern' work environments.

Students interviewed for the SPACE report mentioned above expressed strong preference for the following forms of assessment:

- continuous assessment;
- coursework with discussion;
- personal research projects;
- essay assignments;
- multiple choice.[25]

If they had to do written exams in a set period of time, the students who were interviewed for this project thought that 'open-book' assessments were a better test of their knowledge and skills. Abby Osborne at the University of Bath agrees with this, asserting that good assessments should not simply be about recalling facts.[26] She wonders if there is often too much focus on Bloom's revised taxonomy as a hierarchy. For example, students who find memory recall difficult may in fact be more able than others to demonstrate some higher-order thinking skills, despite not being so strong on levels such as 'remembering' at the base of the taxonomy.

Furthermore, if we have access to digital technology in the real world outside an assessment situation – and the skills to use it appropriately – we can obtain online most of the facts and information that we need to enable us subsequently to 'apply', 'evaluate' and 'create'. Table 14.3 illustrates the taxonomy from the viewpoint of integrating digital tools in teaching and learning. For many students, the wider use of digital tools in education has enabled them to engage more deeply and participate more easily in all levels of the taxonomy.

Table 14.3 Bloom's revised taxonomy with integrated digital tools[27]

Creating	Blogging	Filming	Podcasting	Directing	
Evaluating	Grading	Testing	Posting	Moderating	Higher-order thinking skills
Analysing	Mind-mapping	Surveying	Linking	Validating	
Applying	Calculating	Charting	Editing	Uploading	
Understanding	Noting	Tweeting	Tagging	Subscribing	
Remembering	Bookmarking	Copying	Highlighting	Searching	

Another way of considering how assessments could change to make them more inclusive is to consider whether candidates could be given options to demonstrate what they have learned. London South Bank University is one of a number of higher education institutions to suggest equivalences between types of assessment, as shown in Table 14.4.

Along similar lines, teachers might want to compare how other subjects are assessed and see if there are useful lessons to be learned. In the assessment of languages, for example, there is usually an oral examination. Rather than writing up an experiment, might a student of science give a verbal account of what they did, what took place, and what this proves?

Table 14.4   Assessment equivalences[28]

Assessment	1,000 words equivalent
Examination	1 hour
Essay in foreign language	200–500 words
Group essay	750–1,000 words per group member
Unstructured reflective journal	2,000–3,000 words
Verbal presentation	20 minutes
Group presentation	10 minutes per group member
Clinical/practicum assessment	10 minutes

A further way of permitting greater diversity is to consider *authentic assessment* as part of a course. Authentic assessment allows students to demonstrate that they know a body of knowledge, have developed a set of skills, and can apply them in a 'real-life' situation and solve real-life problems. You may like to look back at **Chapter 2** to consider the validity of authentic assessments and ahead to **Chapter 15** on the role that they could play in the future. It could be argued that authentic assessments not only help assessments to become more accessible, but help us to make better claims about what students know and can do.

Jon Mueller suggests that authenticity in assessment can been seen in a continuum[29] (see Figure 14.1).

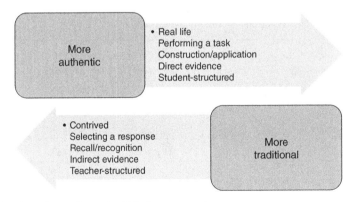

Figure 14.1   A continuum for authenticity in assessment

The National Forum for the Enhancement of Teaching and Learning in Higher Education, in its guide to *Authentic Assessment in Irish Higher Education*, describes the continuum in a graphic that we have simplified in Figure 14.2, which shows how students can find greater ownership, engagement and motivation, as well as learn more, as assessment becomes more authentic.[30]

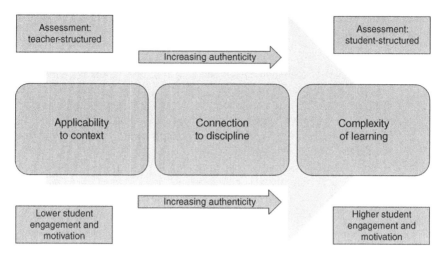

Figure 14.2   Continuum of authentic assessment

Some examples of authentic assessment include the following:

- In business studies, create a strategic plan or showcase for industry, based on real examples.
- In social studies, carry out and analyse interviews alongside a practising health worker.
- In healthcare, create a patient information leaflet.
- In journalism, work to a brief and write a word-limited newspaper article.
- In languages, translate the introduction to a museum guide.

FINAL THOUGHTS

There is still a long way to go before access arrangements, assessment choice or inclusive assessments become common currency. UNESCO says that few countries offer pre- or even in-service training on how to work with students with special needs – and if they do, they tend to focus not on inclusivity, but on contingent or alternative arrangements, thereby singling students out.[51] In many parts of the world, there remains minimal understanding by teachers of how assessment works, let alone how to make assessment inclusive.

The needs of neurodiverse students and the concept of inclusivity have gained enough traction to be part of mainstream thinking in education. Assessment and neurodiversity in practice remains sporadic, but it is getting increasing attention as teachers and assessment organisations see that traditional forms of assessment are not always equitable – and that there are equivalent or different ways of measuring achievement. With more radical thinking, research and professional development, there could be greater opportunities for all – and the exam hall may become less of a default option for how we assess.

KEY TAKEAWAYS

- Neurodiversity is commonly recognised as a trait and should not serve to label or disadvantage students in assessments.
- Inclusive approaches to assessment rely on inclusive approaches to teaching and learning, including with regard to assessment *for* learning and feedback.
- Regulatory bodies and assessment organisations give detailed guidance on access arrangements for assessments.
- Schools and teachers need to support students in their preparations for assessment from a physical, cultural and cognitive perspective.
- Traditional forms of assessment could be rethought so that they become more inclusive while maintaining standards and rigour.

15

ASSESSMENT IN THE FUTURE

IN THIS CHAPTER, YOU WILL:

- consider some of the viewpoints of assessment in today's society;
- look into the future of assessment, considering the themes of how assessment can be made more appropriate, authentic and accessible;
- review some of the innovations that digital technologies may bring.

The assessments that students take today at school-leaving age look broadly the same as those which have been taken for many years. The names of the qualifications mostly sound familiar and methods of assessment have changed little over time. Eighteen-year-olds educated in the English system take A levels, which have been in existence since the middle of the last century; those attending American schools may take the College Board's Advanced Placement exams, which were introduced soon after; the first official International Baccalaureate (IB) Diploma assessments were sat in 1970; and one of the most celebrated school-leaving certificates of them all, the French *baccalauréat*, began life in 1808 under Napoléon Bonaparte.

Change in education is slow because it usually means upheaval – not only in the way that things are done, but also how they are perceived. Even when unexpected external events happen and we consider or hope that they could be a catalyst for change, how we assess students will not become radically different overnight. If what we normally do cannot proceed for operational reasons, we usually apply temporary solutions, from which innovative ways of doing things might be trialled and develop to become mainstream. But it takes considerable thought, prototyping and user-testing before new methods and structures can be put in place.

If recent history has taught us anything, it is that we cannot be certain about the future. What we can do, however, is influence it. As the Russian 1977 Nobel laureate in Chemistry, Ilya Prigogine, is quoted as saying, 'the way to cope with the future is to create it'. In this chapter, we are going to look at a selection of viewpoints about how assessment could look in the future – and what is being done already. First, we will consider why some people think that change in assessment is urgent. We will then look at some proposals for change that have begun to gain currency. And before we conclude, we will explore some of the solutions that digital technologies might have to offer.

CHALLENGES TO CURRENT ASSESSMENT METHODS

Some commentators have criticised the current education system as perpetuating outmoded ways of thinking – a throwback to the Industrial Revolution of the 19th century. Conrad Hughes says that this led to a situation where:

> the scale and implications of schooling became so large that assessment protocols started to act as filters, ensuring that fewer and fewer students would rise to the top of a steep hierarchy of grades, schools, universities, jobs, and titles built to protect elites.[1]

He follows in the footsteps of Ken Robinson, who suggested – with humour – in his famous TED Talk *Do Schools Kill Creativity?* that 'if you were to visit education as an alien and ask "what's it for?" ... you would have to conclude the whole purpose of public education throughout the world is to produce university professors'.[2]

On a more serious note, the British Association of School and College Leaders (ASCL) produced a report showing that 67.1 per cent of students gained a GCSE grade of 4 or above in their exams that year.[3] In their article in the *Times Educational Supplement* reflecting on this evidence and urging change, Bill Lucas and colleagues concluded that 'annually, some 190,000 young people will learn the meaning of the word failure. This is an affront to social justice'.[4]

ASCL's recommendations include improving teacher education and inventing new staged qualifications from primary school upwards, culminating in 'passports' for English and mathematics. Hughes supports 'mastery transcripts',[5] an idea proposed by a consortium of public and private schools mostly in the US, which show what students have achieved at foundational and advanced levels in terms not only of their subject knowledge, but also their transferrable skills, as well as areas including global citizenship and social and emotional literacy.

The Rethinking Assessment movement, led by Lucas and colleagues, similarly suggests that students should receive a 'character scorecard', as well as submitting an extended project qualification at the age of 16 to demonstrate a broader range of knowledge and skills.

They argue for forms of assessment that are more closely aligned to adolescent development. Psychological studies of the teenage brain, such as those being led by Sarah-Jayne Blakemore, professor of psychology and cognitive neuroscience at the University of Cambridge, may inform us when to teach and what to assess. As she wrote in *Inventing Ourselves*, 'knowing whether there are brain-based age windows for learning will be useful when designing lesson plans and educational curricula'.[6]

Richard Elmore, professor of educational leadership at the Harvard Graduate School of Education, in his paper 'The Future of Learning and the Future of Assessment', argues strongly for assessment as a means to provide 'useful information about the development of learners' capabilities', but laments that education processes 'have little to do with learning at the individual or collective level in the broader society. They have more to do with the imperatives of institutional self-interest'.[7] He is concerned about the extent to which schools – and the systems within which they operate – manage so much of children's lives, in terms of attainment, custody and control. In his conception for education that he calls 'Learning 2', he advocates for a situation where:

- *Learning* is the ability to consciously modify understandings, beliefs and actions in response to evidence, experience and reflection.
- *Schooling* is one of many environments in which humans develop the capability to exercise judgement and control over what they learn, how they learn, and what they intend to do with what they have learned.
- *Assessment* is the means by which individuals receive useful information about the development of their capabilities as learners over time.[8]

In some countries, particularly the UK, judgements are made about how well a school is performing based on the proportion of students achieving certain grades in externally marked assessments. This leads to continual pressure on teachers, resulting in stress and fatigue, as well as the 'fear appeals' that we discussed in **Chapter 13**. As we know, the performance of a school is about much more than what is quantifiable, yet it sometimes seems easier to make comparisons – warranted or not – between similar institutions looking only at exam data.

The English assessment organisation AQA, in its report *The future of Assessment*, suggests that there should be an 'assessment ethics framework' involving and agreed by all stakeholders (schools, assessment organisations and government) so that there is greater trust between them with regard to the purpose and use of assessments.[9] Their belief, shared by many, is that assessment should be used to inform teaching and learning, as well as improving schools. David Boud and associates from a number of other universities worldwide stated in one of their provisions for assessment reform for higher education that how and why we assess should be 'subject to continuing dialogue, review and justification within disciplinary and professional communities'.[10]

What we have described in this section are some of the beliefs about assessment as it stands. If we are to challenge assessment methods and design something more universally acceptable, we can work together to debate them in more detail and make changes for the future that will build greater trust and ownership in the system.

CREATING THE FUTURE

What, therefore, is on the table as we aim collectively to create the future of assessment? We have brought some of the current, most prominent ideas together under three headings beginning with the letter 'A': *appropriate*, *authentic* and *accessible*.

APPROPRIATE

In Table 1.1 in **Chapter 1**, we saw that educational assessments may have many purposes, including institution monitoring, organisational intervention and national accounting. It is therefore no surprise that some feel certain that examinations such as GCSEs 'are trying to serve too many masters'.[11] We may determine what the purpose of an assessment is, but it is hard to stop it being put to uses for which it was not originally intended.

The 'washback' effect of assessment has been discussed for many years, with reference to the impact of summative tests on curriculum design and how teachers and learners respond. It can lead to teaching to the test and – where a school's performance is judged on its students' results – a temptation to 'play' the system. Examples of malpractice might include teachers giving students more help with coursework than the rules allow, or students paying others to write assignments for them. Malpractice of this nature has not completely gone away, but strong measures have been taken by regulatory bodies and assessment organisations to counter it.

Rather than looking at assessment as the dominant partner, it may be more beneficial to see it as one part of a pie whose other ingredients are teaching and learning (see Figure 15.1).

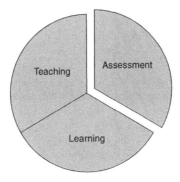

Figure 15.1   The learning, teaching and assessment pie

To inform teaching, we need to assess learning; to assess how well we teach, we should focus on what students are learning; and to know what and how we should be teaching, we should assess and reflect on our own learning. This is why it is fundamental for teachers to have a good understanding of assessment practices, as well as a range of teaching approaches at their disposal to adapt according to what they see and hear from their students. A good teacher will use techniques such as **hinge questions** to find out whether students are still keeping up with what is going on in class – and will have more than one way to continue the lesson from that point depending on what they observe.

Dylan Wiliam points out that any assessment can be used summatively or formatively; these adverbs 'are descriptions of the conclusions we draw from the evidence we get from our assessments'.[12] In a similar way to how teachers will use assessment for learning to adjust what they do in class, a school can use examination results constructively to learn how to improve teaching for future cohorts of students, as discussed in **Chapter 8**.

Anton Béguin and Alison Wood state that 'relatively little consideration has been given to the ways in which summative test results can best be used by teachers and schools formatively, to improve teaching and learning and to inform self-appraisal and evaluation'.[13] They argue that schools need to have access to richer data than they are normally given to deepen their understanding, set meaningful goals, and explain more accurately to stakeholders what they are doing. Their hope is that over time, school inspection and accountability frameworks might evolve to look at how well a school is self-evaluating and setting its own targets for improvement based on multiple forms of evidence.

For assessments of the future to be deemed appropriate, they also need to be manageable for both students and teachers, taken at the appropriate time, and marked in a timely manner. We might question why we put ourselves under such strain and stress in a short period of time when the results of examinations can take a long time to appear – and are consequently not a reflection of the here and now, but rather of the level we reached some weeks or months ago. While appreciating the current logistical and technical complexities, we may want to find ways in which we can be more flexible about how and when assessments are marked so that there is greater immediacy and maybe legitimacy to the results that we receive. We will look at this some more in the sections that follow.

AUTHENTIC

We have already seen in **Chapters 9, 11 and 14** that being able to demonstrate your knowledge and understanding in a real-world environment can be more motivating for students – and sometimes the only legitimate way of assessing their readiness for a future career or vocation. 'Authentic' can also refer to how well assessment methodology has kept up with the world outside the education environment. As Richard Walker put it:

> When students are completing all their formative work digitally it's rather bizarre to be expecting them to sit under examination conditions for three hours or more doing handwritten examinations.[14]

For assessments to be more closely related to what we do when we have left school, it makes sense for them to be designed in collaboration with those who work at the next level – be that universities, employers or perhaps a regulatory body. Lecturers receiving students into their first year of higher education regularly make comparisons of which pre-university qualifications or programmes prepare the new intake better. Research broadly suggests that they want students who have both depth of knowledge in their chosen discipline and the ability to think critically and creatively.[15] Employers may be looking for similar qualities and also proven experience of working successfully in teams or independently (see **Chapters 9 and 10**). Regulatory bodies may want to know that someone can perform a role safely or according to specific standards. The more that school-based assessments can provide evidence of this, the easier it is to recruit at the next level.

This is particularly true with regard to vocational subjects, where there needs to be a means of exemplifying what is hard to assess. In this context, an authentic assessment is one 'that requires students to use the same competencies, or combinations of knowledge, skills and attitudes that they need to apply in the criterion situation in professional life'.[16] Students need to be able to prove that they can put theory into practice. They may be able to describe what needs to be done, but can they actually do it – and thus be seen as more employable?

Prue Huddleston argues that we need to consider three interrelated dimensions when assessing vocational and practical subjects:

- learning that;
- learning how;
- learning where.[17]

She suggests that we need a range of assessment techniques which test more than one dimension at the same time to demonstrate knowledge, skills and application in 'real-life' contexts, whether these are in simulated environments or actually in the kinds of places where students may eventually work. She goes on to echo how much more motivating it is for some students to be assessed in this way, and for this assessment to be carried out in a timely, contextualised way, rather than in unnatural conditions. It may be that disciplines which are less overtly vocational or practical could learn from this.

ACCESSIBLE

In **Chapter 14**, we discussed approaches to teaching, learning and assessment that follow the principles of Universal Design for Learning (UDL). As a reminder, this is a way of creating a new programme or qualification to give all students an opportunity to engage and succeed. In some countries, it is written into working recommendations – if not into law – that activities offered in the public domain need to be made accessible to as many people as possible. We explored accessibility as one property of assessment fairness in **Chapter 4**.

Being accessible often equates to or is partnered with being inclusive. Inclusivity is about permitting access to those who come from historically marginalised backgrounds. This is not only with regard to those who take assessments, but also those who set and mark them. Assessment organisations need to think carefully in the future about the extent to which writers of examination questions are representative of diversity in society, how they can ensure that examiners do not have conscious or unconscious biases, and what could be done in future to prepare and attract those from less proportionally represented sectors to roles in assessment.

Another question related to accessibility is: How much freedom of choice should we allow in examinations to make them more accessible? In future, might we offer a 'pick-and-mix' approach to assessment? Aside from giving students more control to select what appeals to them – and consequently greater motivation – 'optionality', as it is called, allows more coverage of a syllabus in depth. What it can mean, however, as Tom Bramley and Victoria Crisp found with regard to individual examination papers, is that optionality may place greater demands on candidates. This is because they spend time working out which questions will best demonstrate what they know and decipher instructions and rubrics that are potentially more complex.[18] There are greater complexities too with regard to fairness, comparability and the accuracy of marking if some questions are less popular. Making examinations more accessible through optionality may have unintended consequences for accessibility in other aspects of assessment.

DIGITAL TECHNOLOGIES

The digital world has the potential to play a key role in solving many of the issues raised in this chapter. It is not, however, a panacea; and as we stated in the introduction, change in education will not happen overnight. A helpful way to look at how and where digital technology might be used in the future of assessment is first to consider what has been done in the classroom. The education researcher and teacher Ruben Puentedura proposed the 'SAMR' framework:

- *Substitution*: Technology acts as a direct tool substitute, with no functional change.
- *Augmentation*: Technology acts as a direct tool substitute, with functional improvement.
- *Modification*: Technology allows for significant task redesign.
- *Redefinition*: Technology allows for the creation of new tasks, previously inconceivable.[19]

The first two of these could be said to enhance teaching and learning, and the second two to transform it.

As businesses and organisations – not only in the education sector – have met the opportunities and challenges of the digital world, they have often followed a similar staged approach:

- transfer;
- translate;
- transform.

It is the last of these that is potentially the most exciting as it gives the opportunity in educational assessment to begin again using tools that previously did not exist, or to erase bad habits or barriers to accessibility.

To reference again our '3As':

Appropriate

- Digital technologies can gather and analyse richer data for use in classrooms and schools.
- They have the ability to record and measure multiple data points simultaneously, ranging from the time it takes a student to accomplish a task to how much their pulse increases while doing it.
- Certain types of test can be auto-markable. This is especially so for multiple-choice questions, and – with advances in artificial intelligence – may soon be the case for questions that require longer answers.
- Digital technologies can make feedback more immediate so that teachers can adapt their teaching more quickly. This can be especially useful for a large group of students. It is important to remember, however, that a teacher will use their professional knowledge and skills to consider a *range* of aspects in the assessment, learning and subsequent teaching of a student.
- If they are using digital devices, individual candidates could receive a different test to the person sitting next to them. This is often referred to as linear-on-the-fly testing (LOFT). It differs from computerised adaptive testing (CAT) by maintaining the equivalence of the set of items that each candidate sees, whereas CAT is about tailoring an exam to a candidate's ability level according to how well they have performed on previous items.

Authentic

- The use of digital devices in assessment means that candidates can respond to items in ways which are nowadays more familiar to them, such as using a keyboard or other technological means rather than struggling to write legibly by hand.
- The next level of education at university or in a profession is likely to use digital technology in some form, so assessment of how a student can use it 'in action' is a better test of their potential to succeed than using more outmoded methods.
- Digital technologies could allow students to elect when they are ready to test their skills and to do so more than once, with a record kept of their attempts and progression. This could be especially useful for those studying vocational subjects who need, for example, to obtain a qualification before they can use certain tools or machinery.

Accessible

- With digital technologies, current forms of testing could be 'retrofitted' to make them more accessible to some students. This could simply include allowing exams to be sat in more locations or over a longer period of time.
- New forms of assessment, as we have discussed, ought to be designed to be as inclusive as possible. Digital technology has the potential to translate, for example, how we record and assess a candidate's response – perhaps orally rather than in the written form. And it could be transformational in ways yet to be invented or revealed, especially to assist in the assessment of complex interactive tasks.

For many forms of assessment, technology enables examiners to work wherever is most convenient to them. It opens up more options for assessment organisations to recruit examiners wherever in the world they live. Many examination papers are already scanned and marked online. As we saw in **Chapter 6**, this also means that assessment organisations can more easily monitor the work of examiners.

There are, of course, questions of security when technology is being used in the administration or marking of assessment, and it is a priority of education organisations to ensure that this is taken fully into consideration. Elements need to be in place, such as remote proctoring, which aims to ensure the integrity of an exam by requiring students to confirm their identity – perhaps through a fingerprint or an iris scan – and then monitoring each individual while they are taking an assessment through video or movement to look for any behaviour that could indicate cheating. And we must not presume that everyone everywhere in the world has the same access to technology or secure systems.

We may expect that young people would prefer to take assessments that are digital in some form, but this is not always the case. Gavin Brown found that the use of technology in assessment can lead to students initially being excited by novel methods, but being concerned at how well they will perform if they have not had much opportunity to practise with them.[20] Students may 'retreat' to the tried-and-tested methods with which they (and their teachers and parents) are more familiar. Some students have also expressed concerns about how data that have been collated about them will be used – and for how long they will be held. They need reassurances that their performance or behaviour when they were still learning and less mature is not held against them by future tutors or employers.

And we need to bear in mind the credence that those who understand less about new methods of assessment will give to them. As Chris Cobb, pro-vice chancellor and deputy chief executive of the University of London, says:

> Digital assessment offers immense opportunities to improve student experience and develop modes of assessment which are more relevant and aligned to today's needs. However, it also carries risk and it will be important that change is iterative and paced to ensure quality and maintain public confidence in qualification standards.[21]

FINAL THOUGHTS

Disruptions to normal systems and protocols of assessment in recent times have given us pause to reflect and opportunities to try out new methodologies. In some cases, they have forced assessment organisations to advance and action their thinking much more rapidly than they might otherwise have done. There are many risks involved in introducing new forms of assessment, but there are also business risks in not reacting quickly enough – even if initially only in a tactical rather than a strategic way.

Some key points to remember are that the future of assessment will be dependent on a range of factors which deserve careful thought and attention. Some of the traditions of assessment might appear outdated, but they are often the result of many years of experience and expertise in maintaining validity, reliability and standards. Assessments need to be fit for the purposes for which they are intended, maintain principles, use a common language, and be recognised by other levels of education, employers and the general public. Assessment organisations cannot work in isolation to achieve this.

It is also clear that to inform the argument of what assessment should look like in the future, we need to improve teachers' and school leaders' understanding of it. We hope that this book will go some way to realising this aim. It is incumbent on us, as professionals working in teaching, learning and assessment, to equip ourselves with the best tools to enable students to fulfil and demonstrate their potential.

KEY TAKEAWAYS

- Transformation in education assessment should be a considered process.
- New forms of assessment will need to prove their validity, reliability and standards, as well as being recognised by those who need to know an individual's readiness for further education or employment.
- Digital technologies, other tools and creative thinking may help us to make assessments more appropriate, authentic and accessible.
- To enable teachers and school leaders to be properly involved in creating the future of assessment, we should provide opportunities for continued professional development (CPD).
- The ways that we assess, teach and help students to learn are integral to their future lives.

GLOSSARY

A level – Also known as 'advanced level', a subject-based qualification offered to students completing secondary or pre-university education. A levels were introduced in England and Wales and have since been adopted in a range of jurisdictions, including Kenya, Singapore and Zimbabwe. The A level is a primary qualification for university entry.

assessment objectives (AOs) – The knowledge, skills and understanding that an assessment-taker needs to demonstrate through their responses to assessment tasks and items. Individual items in an assessment may be linked to one or more assessment objectives.

claim – A statement that something is the case, typically without providing evidence or proof. In educational assessment, validation practice is the collection of empirical or theoretical evidence to establish whether claims to validity can be warranted.

classical test theory (CTT) – A branch of psychometrics that is concerned with improving the validity and reliability of assessments. CTT assumes that each person has an innate true score (i.e. their ability on a scale related to a trait). This can be summarised by the equation below:

$$X = T + E$$

where:

- X is an observed score;
- T is the true score;
- E is random error.

Various statistics can be used in CTT to determine the quality of the assessment as a measure of the targeted trait. One of the statistics used is the standard error of measurement (SEm), which is a measure of how scores on an assessment are spread around a true score.

construct – A proposed attribute of a person that can be measured through accumulation of assessment evidence. Constructs can either be directly measurable (e.g. height) or indirectly measurable (e.g. mathematical ability). For indirect constructs, a series of tasks or items must be developed that target the behavioural manifestations of the construct. In practice, constructs are defined through documentation such as curricula, learning objectives, grading descriptors and assessment objectives.

cut score – A selected point on the scale of the assessment that aims to differentiate between different ability levels of assessment-takers. Cut scores reflect a judgement from qualified practitioners or subject experts.

double marking – Where more than one examiner reaches a judgement about a submitted response to an assessment. The final mark given to the student is typically a combination of the two given marks. Multiple marking is when more than two examiners are used.

General Certificate of Secondary Education (GCSE) – An academic qualification taken in England, Wales and Northern Ireland. It is normally taken at the end of compulsory schooling at age 15 or 16. GCSEs are offered in a range of subjects, and the majority of students take between 8 and 11 GCSEs.

grade descriptors – An overall statement about the standards that need to be reached in a subject discipline or qualification to achieve a particular grade outcome. They aim to define the requirements of a qualification and the main learning outcomes, and can inform the development of assessment objectives.

grade inflation – The real or claimed increase of grade outcomes of consecutive cohorts. Grade inflation is considered an issue for standards if there is evidence to suggest that students of the same ability are receiving different grade outcomes on the basis of their cohort.

hinge question – A question that can be used in a lesson to diagnose how much students know or understand about a topic, as well as what a teacher should do next.

item – The 'catch-all' term for both the assessment task (e.g. the question) and the associated mark scheme (or rubric). It is recommended that all of the component parts of an item, such as stimulus materials, the assessment task or question, and the mark scheme, are developed at the same time and reviewed simultaneously.

item characteristic curves (ICCs) – Also known as item response curves, ICCs are used to describe the relationship between the ability, defined on an *ability* scale, and each item in an assessment. ICCs plot the probability of assessment-takers correctly answering an item based on their ability. As ability increases, the probability of correctly answering the item also increases. The shape of an ICC plot determines both the difficulty and the discriminatory properties of an item.

item response theory (IRT) – Also known as *latent trait theory*, IRT is a theory of testing based on the relationship between individuals' performances on a test item and the assessment-takers' levels of performance on an overall measure of the ability that item was designed to measure. IRT statistical methods aim to establish a link between the properties of items on an assessment or instrument, assessment-takers responding to the items, and the underlying trait being measured. IRT is based on the idea that the probability of a correct response to an item is a mathematical function of person and item parameters.

Similar to classical test theory (CTT), IRT is used in the design, scoring and analysis of assessments. Compared to CTT, IRT brings greater flexibility and provides more sophisticated information. For example, it can provide more precise predictions for whether students of differing ability levels will answer a particular item correctly or not.

IRT has many applications in educational assessment, including but not limited to providing a framework for the evaluation of item performance, maintaining banks of items (e.g. by analysing whether items within a bank have become overexposed), and using item banks to create assessments of equivalent demand.

Key Stage 3 – Three years of schooling in government-funded schools in England, Wales and Northern Ireland. Students in Key Stage 3 are aged between 11 and 14. This stage normally covers the first three years of secondary education and defines the group of pupils who undertake the national curriculum.

measurement error – The difference between a measured value of a quantity and its true value. Measurement error may come from a variety of different sources. Human measurement error can occur in all stages of assessment design, including during marking. Systematic errors may occur when there are issues in the setting or administration of the assessment. Error can also be random (i.e. from an unknown source).

national curriculum levels – The grading system used and applied by schools in England and Wales until 2014 for students up to 14 years old. There were eight levels in total, which represented progression until the end of Key Stage 3. Large-scale assessments were conducted for students when they reached the end of defined Key Stages, which provided an overall statement of their attainment.

National Student Survey (NSS) – A survey that is offered to undergraduate students in the UK, taken by approximately half a million students per year. The NSS is used to gather student views on the quality of their university courses and their overall educational experiences.

No Child Left Behind – The main law for K–12 general education in the US from 2002 to 2015. The law held schools accountable for how children learned and achieved. It required all public schools receiving federal funding to deliver standardised tests annually to all students.

Office of Qualifications and Examinations Regulation (Ofqual) – A non-ministerial government department based in England. It is responsible for the maintenance of standards and instilling public confidence in qualifications and assessment. It is the authority that accredits and regulates assessment organisations offering high-stakes qualifications.

pedagogical content knowledge – The knowledge that teachers develop over time and through experience about how to teach content in particular ways in order to lead to learning. A teacher's pedagogical content knowledge is influenced by their breadth of experience, the specifics of the content that they are teaching, and their teaching environment.

qualitative data – Data that are descriptive in nature, and therefore can be observed but not measured. An example of qualitative data is language.

quantitative data – Information about quantities – observations can be quantified using numbers. Data can either be counted or compared on a numeric scale.

REFERENCES

INTRODUCTION

1. Department for Education (DfE). (2019). *Early career framework*. https://assets.publishing.service. gov.uk/government/uploads/system/uploads/attachment_data/file/913646/Early-Career_ Framework.pdf
2. Welsh Government. (2017). *Professional standards for teaching and leadership*. https://hwb.gov. wales/api/storage/19bc948b-8a3f-41e0-944a-7bf2cadf7d18/professional-standards-for-teaching-and-leadership-interactive-pdf-for-pc.pdf
3. Centre for Education and Youth (CFEY). (2020). *Making waves: Building a better future for assessment*. https://cfey.org/reports/2020/12/making-waves-building-a-better-future-for-assessment-final-report/

CHAPTER 1

1. Black, P., & Wiliam, D. (1998). Inside the black box: Raising standards through classroom assessment. *Phi Delta Kappan, 80*(2), 139–148.
2. Bennett, R. E. (2011). Formative assessment: A critical review. *Assessment in Education: Principles, Policy & Practice, 18*(1), 5–25.
3. Black, P., & Wiliam, D. (2009). Developing a theory of formative assessment. *Educational Assessment, Evaluation and Accountability, 21*(1), 5–31.
4. Newton, P. E. (2007). Clarifying the purposes of educational assessment. *Assessment in Education: Principles, Policy & Practice, 14*(2), 149–170.
5. Strathern, M. (1997). Audit in the British university system. *European Review, 5*(3), 305–321.
6. Newberg-Long, D. (2010). *Narrowing of curriculum: Teaching in an age of accountability* [PhD thesis, University of Denver]. Digital Commons @ DU. https://digitalcommons.du.edu/etd/892
7. Newton, P. E. (2017). There is more to educational measurement than measuring: The importance of embracing purpose pluralism. *Educational Measurement: Issues and Practice, 36*(2), 5–15.

CHAPTER 2

1. Messick, S. (1989). Validity. In R. L. Linn (Ed.), *Educational measurement* (3rd ed., pp. 13–103). Macmillan. (p. 13)
2. Stobart, G., & Gipps, C. V. (1997). *Assessment: A teacher's guide to the issues*. Hodder & Stoughton.

3. Department for Education (DfE). (2013). *Geography programmes of study: Key Stage 3.* https://assets.publishing.service.gov.uk/government/uploads/system/uploads/attachment_data/file/239087/SECONDARY_national_curriculum_-_Geography.pdf

4. Ibid.

5. Messick, S. (1998). Alternative modes of assessment, uniform standards of validity. In M. Hakel (Ed.), *Beyond multiple choice: Evaluating alternatives to traditional testing for selection* (pp. 59–74). Lawrence Erlbaum Associates.

6. Kane, M. T. (2013). Validating the interpretations and uses of test scores. *Journal of Educational Measurement, 50*(1), 1–73.

7. Kane, M. T. (1992). An argument-based approach to validity. *Psychological Bulletin, 112*(3), 527–535.

8. Shaw, S. D., & Crisp, V. (2015). Reflections on a framework for validation – five years on. *Research Matters, 19,* 31–37.

9. Gill, T., & Vidal Rodeiro, C. L. (2014). *Predictive validity of level 3 qualifications: Extended Project, Cambridge Pre-U, International Baccalaureate, BTEC Diploma.* Cambridge Assessment.

10. Vidal Rodeiro, C. L., & Zanini, N. (2015). The role of the A* grade at A level as a predictor of university performance in the United Kingdom. *Oxford Review of Education, 41*(5), 647–670. https://doi.org/10.1080/03054985.2015.1090967

CHAPTER 3

1. Moskal, B. M., & Leydens, J. A. (2000). Scoring rubric development: Validity and reliability. *Practical Assessment Research & Evaluation, 7*(10), 1–6. https://doi.org/10.7275/q7rm-gg74 (p. 5)

2. Stock, P. (2017). *Principles of great assessment #3: Reliability.* https://joeybagstock.wordpress.com/2017/05/03/principles-of-great-assessment-3-reliability/

3. Tisi, J., Whitehouse, G., Maughan, S., & Burdett, N. (2013). *A review of literature on marking reliability.* https://assets.publishing.service.gov.uk/government/uploads/system/uploads/attachment_data/file/605688/0613_JoTisi_et_al-nfer-a-review-of-literature-on-marking-reliability.pdf (p. 8)

4. Stobart, G. (2008). *Testing times: The uses and abuses of assessment.* Routledge.

5. Ofqual. (2013). *Introduction to the concept of reliability.* https://www.gov.uk/government/publications/reliability-of-assessment-compendium/introduction-to-the-concept-of-reliability

6. Ahmed, A., & Pollitt, A. (2011). Improving marking quality through a taxonomy of mark schemes. *Assessment in Education: Principles, Policy & Practice, 18*(3), 259–278. https://doi.org/10.1080/0969594X.2010.546775

7. Ofqual. (2016). *An investigation into the 'Sawtooth Effect' in GCSE and AS/A level assessments.* https://assets.publishing.service.gov.uk/government/uploads/system/uploads/attachment_data/file/549686/an-investigation-into-the-sawtooth-effect-in-gcse-as-and-a-level-assessments.pdf

8. Wiliam, D. (2001). Reliability, validity, and all that jazz. *Education, 29*(3), 17–21. https://doi.org/10.1080/03004270185200311

9. Tisi et al. (2013). op. cit.

10. Nadas, R., & Suto, I. (2011). *Assessing the Extended Project Qualification: A model of early challenges for marking accuracy.* Cambridge Assessment.

11. Warrens, M. J. (2015). On Cronbach's alpha being the mean of all split-half reliabilities. In R. E. Millsap., D. M. Bolt., L. A. van der Ark., & W. C. Wang. (Eds.), *Proceedings of the 78th Meeting of the Psychometric Society* (pp. 293–300). Springer.

12. Bramley, T. (2007). Quantifying marker agreement: Terminology, statistics and issues. *Research Matters, 4*, 22–28.

13. Salkind, N. J. (2010). *Encyclopaedia of research design.* SAGE.

14. Bramley, T. (2001). The question tariff problem in GCSE mathematics. *Evaluation & Research in Education, 15*(2), 95–107.

15. Suto, I., & Greatorex, J. (2008). What goes through an examiner's mind? Using verbal protocols to gain insights into the GCSE marking process. *British Educational Research Journal, 34*(2), 213–233.

16. Suto, I., & Nadas, R. (2008). What determines GCSE marking accuracy? An exploration of expertise among maths and physics markers. *Research Papers in Education, 23*(4), 477–497.

17. Child, S. F. J., Munro, J., & Benton, T. (2015). *An experimental investigation of the effects of mark scheme features on marking reliability.* https://www.cambridgeassessment.org.uk/Images/417277-an-experimental-investigation-of-the-effects-of-mark-scheme-features-on-marking-reliability.pdf

18. Hughes, S. & Shaw, S. D. (2016). Why do so few candidates score 4 out of 8 on this question? The issue of under-used marks in levels-based mark schemes. *Research Matters, 21*, 42–48.

19. He, Q., Hayes, M., & Wiliam, D. (2011). *Classification accuracy in results from Key Stage 2 national curriculum tests.* Ofqual.

20. Wheadon, C., & Stockford, I. (2010). *Classification accuracy and consistency in GCSE and A level examinations offered by the Assessment and Qualifications Alliance (AQA) November 2008 to June 2009.* AQA.

CHAPTER 4

1. Nisbet, I., & Shaw, S. D. (2020). *Is assessment fair?* SAGE.

2. Tierney, R. D. (2013). Fairness in classroom assessment. In J. H. McMillan (Ed.), *Handbook of research on classroom assessment* (pp. 124–144). SAGE.

3. Isaacs, T., Zara, C., Herbert, G., Coombs, S.J., & Smith, C. (2013). *Key concepts in educational assessment.* SAGE. (p. 57)

4. Equality and Human Rights Commission. (2020). *Protected characteristics.* https://www.equality-humanrights.com/en/equality-act/protected-characteristics

5. Nisbet, N., & Shaw, S. D. (2019). Fair assessment viewed through the lenses of measurement theory. *Assessment in Education: Principles, Policy & Practice, 26*(5), 612–629. https://doi.org/10.1080/0969594X.2019.1586643

6. American Educational Research Association (AERA), American Psychological Association (APA), & National Council on Measurement in Education (NCME). (2014). *Standards for educational and psychological testing.* AERA.

7. Barrance, R. (2019). The fairness of internal assessment in the GCSE: The value of students' accounts. *Assessment in Education: Principles, Policy and Practice, 26*(5), 563–583.

8. Popham, W. J. (2012). *Assessment bias: How to banish it.* Pearson.

9. McMillan, J. H. (2008). *Assessment essentials for standards-based education.* Corwin.

10. Kelly, S., & Dennick, R. (2009). Evidence of gender bias in True-False-Abstain medical examinations. *BMC Medical Education, 9*(32). https://doi.org/10.1186/1472-6920-9-32

11. Bond, A., Bodger, O., Skibinski, D., Jones, D., Restall, C., Dudley, E., & van Keulen, G. (2013). Negatively-marked MCQ assessments that reward partial knowledge do not introduce gender bias yet increase student performance and satisfaction and reduce anxiety. *PloS One, 8*(2), e55956. https://doi.org/10.1371/journal.pone.0055956

12. Gawande, A. (2010). *The checklist manifesto: How to get things right.* Picador.
13. Hambleton, R., & Rodgers, J. H. (1995). Item bias review. *Practical Assessment Research & Evaluation, 4*(6), 1–3.
14. Crisp, V. (2011). Exploring features that affect the difficulty and functioning of science exam questions for those with reading difficulties. *Irish Educational Studies, 30*(3), 323–343. (p. 323)
15. Hanna, E. I. (2005). *Inclusive design for maximum accessibility: A practical approach to universal design.* http://images.pearsonassessments.com/images/tmrs/tmrs_rg/RR_05_04.pdf
16. Bramley, T. (2005). Accessibility, easiness and standards. *Educational Research, 47*(2), 251–261.
17. Pollitt, A., Ahmed, A., & Crisp, V. (2007). The demands of examination syllabuses and question papers. In P. Newton, J.-A. Baird, H. Goldstein, H. Patrick, & P. Tymms (Eds.), *Techniques for monitoring the comparability of examination standards* (pp. 166–211). QCA.
18. Joint Council for Qualifications (JCQ). (2020). *Access arrangements, reasonable adjustments and special consideration.* https://www.jcq.org.uk/exams-office/access-arrangements-and-special-consideration/
19. Beddow, P. A., Elliott, S. N., & Kettler, R. J. (2013). Test accessibility: Item reviews and lessons learned from four state assessments. *Education Research International, 2013,* 1–12.
20. Qualifications Wales and Council for the Curriculum, Examinations & Assessment (CCEA). (2015). *Fair access by design.* https://www.qualificationswales.org/media/4739/fair-access-by-design.pdf
21. Lonsdale, M. D. S. (2014). The effect of text layout on performance: A comparison between types of questions that require different reading processes. *Information Design Journal, 21*(3), 279–299.
22. Cawthon, S., Leppo, R., Carr, T., & Kopriva, R. (2013). Towards accessible assessments: The promises and limitations of item test adaptations for students with disabilities and English language learners. *Educational Assessment, 18*(2), 73–98.
23. Sireci, S. G. (2004). *Validity issues in accommodating NAEP reading tests* [Paper presentation]. NABG Conference on Increasing the Participation of SD and LEP Students in NAEP.
24. Bramley. (2005). op. cit.
25. Ibid.
26. Gipps, C., & Stobart, G. (2009). Fairness in assessment. In C. Wyatt-Smith & J. Cumming (Eds.), *Educational assessment in the 21st century* (pp. 105–118). Springer.
27. Rasooli, A., Zandi, H., & DeLuca, C. (2019). Conceptualising fairness in classroom assessment: Exploring the value of organisational justice theory. *Assessment in Education: Principles, Policy & Practice, 26*(5), 584–611.

CHAPTER 5

1. Richmond, T. (2018). *A degree of uncertainty: An investigation into grade inflation at universities.* http://www.tom-richmond.com/wp-content/uploads/2018/06/A%20Degree%20of%20Uncertainty.pdf
2. Baird, J., Isaacs, T., Opposs, D., & Gray, L. (Eds.). (2018). *Examination standards: How measures & meanings differ around the world.* UCL IOE Press.
3. Gray, L., & Baird, J.-A. (2020). Systemic influences on standard setting in national examinations. *Assessment in Education: Principles, Policy & Practice, 27*(2), 137–141. https://doi.org/10.1080/0969594X.2020.1750116
4. Burdett, N., Houghton, E., Sargent, C., & Tisi, J. (2013). *Maintaining qualification and assessment standards: Summary of international practice.* https://assets.publishing.service.gov.uk/government/

uploads/system/uploads/attachment_data/file/605860/0113_NewmanBurdett_Maintaining_qualifi
cation_and_assessment_standards_V4_FINAL.pdf

5. Pollitt, A., Ahmed, A., & Crisp, V. (2007). The demands on examination syllabuses and question papers. In P. Newton., J.-A. Baird, H. Goldstein., H. Patrick., & P. Tymms. (Eds.), *Techniques for monitoring the comparability of examination standards* (pp. 166–206). QCA.

6. Johnson, M., & Mehta, S. (2011). Evaluating the CRAS framework: Development and recommendations. *Research Matters*, *12*, 27–33.

7. Pollitt, A., Hughes, A., Ahmed, A., Fisher-Hoch, H., & Bramley, T. (1998). *The effects of structure on the demands in GCSE and A level questions*. QCA.

8. Cizek, G. J. (1993). Reconsidering standards and criteria. *Journal of Educational Measurement*, *30*(2), 93–106.

9. Ibid. (p. 100)

10. Cizek, G. J. (Ed.). (2001). *Setting performance standards: Concepts, methods and perspectives*. Erlbaum.

11. Bramley, T. (2012, March 28). *What if the grade boundaries on all A level examinations were set at a fixed proportion of the total mark?* [Paper presentation]. Maintaining Examination Standards Seminar, London.

12. Richmond. (2018). op. cit.

13. Ricker, K. (2006). Setting cut-scores: A critical review of the Angoff and modified Angoff methods. *Alberta Journal of Educational Research*, *52*(1), 53–64.

14. Baird, J.-A. (2007). Alternative conceptions of comparability. In P. Newton, J.-A. Baird, H. Goldstein, H. Patrick, & P. Tymms (Eds.), *Techniques for monitoring the comparability of examination standards* (pp. 124–165). QCA.

15. Bramley, T., & Wilson, F. (2016). Maintaining test standards by expert judgement of item difficulty. *Research Matters*, *21*, 48–54.

16. Tong, C.-S., Lee, C., & Luo, G. (2020). Assessment reform in Hong Kong: Developing the HKDSE to align with the new academic structure. *Assessment in Education: Principles, Policy & Practice*, *27*(2), 232–248. https://doi.org/10.1080/0969594X.2020.1732866

17. National Foundation for Educational Research (NFER). (2020). *What is the National Reference Test?* https://www.nfer.ac.uk/for-schools/free-resources-advice/assessment-hub/introduction-to-assess ment/understanding-the-national-reference-test/

18. Wetton, C., Hopkins, A., & Benson, L. (2019). *National Reference Test results digest*. NFER.

19. Ibid.

20. Ofqual. (2019). *NRT annual statement 2019*. https://assets.publishing.service.gov.uk/government/ uploads/system/uploads/attachment_data/file/826570/NRT_annual_statement_2019__-_ FINAL196527.pdf

21. Torrance, H. (2018). The return to final paper examining in English national curriculum assessment and school examinations: Issues of validity, accountability and politics. *British Journal of Educational Studies*, *66*(1), 3–27. https://doi.org/10.1080/00071005.2017.1322683

22. Nisbet, I. (2014, November 6–8). *What is meant by 'rigour' in examinations?* [Paper presentation]. 40th Conference of the International Association for Educational Assessment, Tallinn, Estonia.

CHAPTER 6

1. Johnson, M., Crisp, V., & Constantinou, F. (2017). How do question writers compose external examination questions? Question writing as a socio-cognitive process. *British Educational Research Journal*, *43*(4), 700–719.

2. Johnson, M., & Rushton, N. (2019). A culture of question writing: Professional examination question writers' practices. *Educational Research, 61*(2), 197–213. https://doi.org/10.1080/00131881.2019.1600378

3. OCR. (2020). *Assessment specialist – assessment analyst.* https://www.ocr.org.uk/Images/421463-assessment-analyst-task-descriptor.pdf

4. OCR. (2016). *Ten key stats about examining.* https://www.ocr.org.uk/Images/302850-ocr-s-ten-key-stats-about-examining.pdf

5. Black, B. (2015). *Marking and grading.* https://ocr.org.uk/Images/142042-marking-and-grading-assuring-ocr-s-accuracy.pdf

6. Benton, T. (2016). *Comparable outcomes: Scourge or scapegoat?* https://www.cambridgeassessment.org.uk/Images/346267-comparable-outcomes-scourge-or-scapegoat-.pdf

7. Ofqual. (2014). *Setting GCSE, AS level and A level standards in Summer 2014 and 2015.* https://assets.publishing.service.gov.uk/government/uploads/system/uploads/attachment_data/file/451321/2015-08-05-summer-series-gcse-as-and-a-level-grade-standards.pdf

8. Wiliam, D. (1996). Standards in examinations: a matter of trust? *The Curriculum Journal, 7*(3), 293–306. (p. 304)

CHAPTER 7

1. Vitello, S., & Williamson, J. (2017). Internal vs external assessment in vocational qualifications: A commentary on government reforms in England. *London Review of Education, 15*(3). https://doi.org/10.18546/LRE.15.3.14

2. Maxwell, G. (2006, May). *Quality management of school-based assessments: Moderation of teacher judgements* [Paper presentation]. 32nd IAEA Conference, Singapore.

3. Williamson, J., & Child, S. F. J. (2018, September). *How can mark scheme design support valid and reliable school-based assessment?* [Paper presentation]. European Conference of Educational Research, Bolzano, Italy.

4. Black, B., Suto, I., & Bramley, T. (2011). The interrelations of features of questions, mark schemes and examinee responses and their impact upon marker agreement. *Assessment in Education: Principles, Policy & Practice, 18*(3), 295–318.

5. Maxwell. (2006). op. cit.

6. Adie, L. E. (2009). Changing assessment practices: The case for online moderation. In P. Jeffrey (Ed.), *Proceedings of the Australian Association for Research in Education 2008 International Educational Research Conference* (pp. 1–14). Australian Association for Research in Education.

7. Bloxham, S., Hughes, C., & Adie, L. (2016). What's the point of moderation? A discussion of the purposes achieved through contemporary moderation practices. *Assessment & Evaluation in Higher Education, 41*(4), 638–653. https://doi.org/10.1080/02602938.2015.1039932

8. Sadler, D. R. (2011). Academic freedom, achievement standards and professional identity. *Quality in Higher Education, 17*(1), 85–100.

9. Smaill, E. (2020). Using involvement in moderation to strengthen teachers' assessment for learning capability. *Assessment in Education: Principles, Policy & Practice.* https://doi.org/10.1080/0969594X.2020.1777087

10. National Foundation for Educational Research (NFER). (2019). *Moderation of teacher judgements.* https://www.nfer.ac.uk/media/3139/moderation_of_assessment_judgements.pdf

11. Watty, K., Freeman, M., Howieson, B., Hancock, P., O'Connell, B., de Lange, P., & Abraham, A. (2014). Social moderation, assessment and assuring standards for accounting graduates. *Assessment & Evaluation in Higher Education, 39*(4), 461–478.

12. Crisp, V. (2018). Insights into teacher moderation of marks on high-stakes non-examined assessments. *Research Matters, 25*, 13–20.

13. Bloxham, S., & Boyd, P. (2007). *Developing effective assessment in higher education: A practical guide.* McGraw Hill International.

14. Hipkins, R., & Robertson, S. (2011). *Moderation and teacher learning: What can research tell us about their interrelationships?* New Zealand Council for Educational Research.

15. Smaill. (2020). op. cit.

16. Luke, A., Weir, K., & Woods, A. (2008). *Development of a set of principles to guide a P-12 syllabus framework: A report delivered to the Queensland Studies Authority.* Queensland Studies Authority.

17. Smaill. (2020). op. cit.

18. Sadler, D. R. (1989). Formative assessment and the design of instructional systems. *Instructional Science, 18*(2), 119–144.

19. Whitehouse, C., & Pollitt, A. (2012). *Using adaptive comparative judgement to obtain a highly reliable rank order in summative assessment.* https://filestore.aqa.org.uk/content/research/CERP_RP_CW_20062012_2.pdf?download=1

20. Brooks, V. (2012). Marking as judgment. *Research Papers in Education, 27*(1), 63–80.

21. Raikes, N., Scorey, S., & Shiell, H. (2008, September). *Grading examinations using expert judgements from a diverse pool of judges* [Paper presentation]. 34th Annual Conference of the International Association for Educational Assessment, Cambridge.

22. Pollitt, A. (2012). Comparative judgement for assessment. *International Journal of Technology and Design Education, 22*(2), 157–170.

23. Tarricone, P., & Newhouse, C. P. (2016). Using comparative judgement and online technologies in the assessment and measurement of creative performance and capability. *International Journal of Educational Technology in Higher Education, 13.* https://doi.org/10.1186/s41239-016-0018-x (p. 3)

24. Bramley, T. (2007). Paired comparison methods. In P. Newton, J.-A. Baird, H. Goldstein, H. Patrick, & P. Tymms (Eds.), *Techniques for monitoring the comparability of examination standards* (pp. 246–294). QCA.

25. Laming, D. (2004). *Human judgment: The eye of the beholder.* Cengage. (p. 9)

26. Suto, I., & Greatorex, J. (2008). What goes through an examiner's mind? Using verbal protocols to gain insights into the GCSE marking process. *British Educational Research Journal, 34*(2), 213–233. https://doi.org/10.1080/01411920701492050

27. Ofqual. (2018). *Marking reliability studies 2017: Rank ordering versus marking – Which is more reliable?* Ofqual.

28. McMahon, S., & Jones, I. (2014). A comparative judgement approach to teacher assessment. *Assessment in Education: Principles, Policy & Practice.* https://doi.org/10.1080/0969594X.2014.978839

29. Bramley, T., & Vitello, S. (2019). The effect of adaptivity on the reliability coefficient in adaptive comparative judgement. *Assessment in Education: Principles, Policy & Practice, 26*(1), 43–58.

30. Ibid.

31. Bramley, T. (2015). *Investigating the reliability of adaptive comparative judgement.* Cambridge Assessment.

32. Whitehouse & Pollitt. (2012). op. cit.

33. Bramley. (2015). op. cit.

34. Bramley & Vitello. (2019). op. cit. (p. 45)

35. Curcin, M., Howard, E., Sully, K., & Black, B. (2019). *Improving awarding: 2018/19 pilots.* https://dera.ioe.ac.uk/34720/1/Improving_awarding_-_FINAL196575.pdf

36. Wheadon, C., Barmby, P., Christodoulou, D., & Henderson, B. (2020). A comparative judgement approach to the large-scale assessment of primary writing in England. *Assessment in Education: Principles, Policy & Practice, 27*(1), 46–64. https://doi.org/10.1080/0969594X.2019.1700212

37. Barmby, P., Christodoulou, D., Defty, N., Henderson, B., & Wheadon, C. (2019, November 13–16). *Judges' considerations in assessing children's writing in a comparative judgement process* [Paper presentation]. Association for Educational Assessment Europe Annual Conference, Lisbon, Portugal.

38. Christodoulou, D. (2017). *Using comparative judgement to measure progress.* https://blog.nomoremarking.com/using-comparative-judgement-to-measure-progress-131ca30eb9bc

CHAPTER 8

1. National College for Teaching and Leadership (NCTL). (2014). *Beyond levels: Alternative assessment approaches developed by teaching in schools.* https://assets.publishing.service.gov.uk/government/uploads/system/uploads/attachment_data/file/349266/beyond-levels-alternative-assessment-approaches-developed-by-teaching-schools.pdf

2. Organisation for Economic Co-operation and Development (OECD). (2009). *Assessment for learning: Formative assessment.* OECD.

3. Brown, G. T. L. (2017). The future of assessment as a human and social endeavor: Addressing the inconvenient truth of error. *Frontiers in Education, 2*(3). https://doi.org/10.3389/feduc.2017.00003

4. Magno, C. (2009). Demonstrating the difference between classical test theory and item response theory using derived test data. *International Journal of Educational and Psychological Assessment, 1*(1), 1–11.

5. Didau, D. (2019). *How do we know that students are making progress? Part 1: The problems with flight paths.* https://learningspy.co.uk/assessment/how-do-we-know-pupils-are-marking-progress-part-1-the-problem-with-flightpaths/

6. Wiliam, D. (2009). *Assessment for learning: Why, what and how.* UCL Institute of Education.

7. Christodoulou, D. (2016). *Making good progress? The future of assessment for learning.* Oxford University Press.

8. Timperley, H. (2009). Using assessment data for improving teaching practice. *Australian College of Educators, 8*(3), 21–27. https://research.acer.edu.au/cgi/viewcontent.cgi?article=1036&context=research_conference

9. Mandinach, E. B., & Gummer, E. (2016). What does it mean for teachers to be data literate: Laying out the skills, knowledge and dispositions. *Teaching and Teacher Education, 60.* https://doi.org/10.1016/j.tate.2016.07.011

CHAPTER 9

1. Suto, I. (2013). 21st Century skills: Ancient, ubiquitous, enigmatic? *Research Matters, 15,* 2–8. https://www.cambridgeassessment.org.uk/Images/467763-21st-century-skills-ancient-ubiquitous-enigmatic-.pdf (p. 3)

2. Assessment and Teaching of 21st Century Skills (ATC21S). (n.d.). *About the project.* http://www.atc21s.org

3. Schleicher, A. (2010). *The case for 21st-century learning*. https://www.oecd.org/general/thecase-for21st-centurylearning.htm

4. Ibid.

5. Cambridge Assessment International Education. (2020). *Implementing the curriculum with Cambridge: A guide for school leaders*. https://www.cambridgeinternational.org/Images/134557-implementing-the-curriculum-with-cambridge.pdf

6. Cambridge Assessment International Education. (2019). *Cambridge IGCSE (9-1) physical education 0995 syllabus*. https://www.cambridgeinternational.org/Images/557055-2022-2024-syllabus.pdf

7. International Baccalaureate Organization (IBO). (2015). *Diploma Programme subject brief: Creativity, action and service (CAS)*. https://www.ibo.org/contentassets/5895a05412144fe890312bad52b17044/cas-2016-english-1st-final-web.pdf

8. Ibid.

9. Ibid.

10. International Baccalaureate Organization (IBO). (2017). *Research snapshot: The impact of creativity, action, service (CAS) on students and communities*. https://www.ibo.org/globalassets/publications/ib-research/dp/cas-snapshot-2017-en.pdf

11. McIntosh, S. (2018). *The enduring impact of creativity, activity, service (CAS) in the IB Diploma Programme: The alumni study*. https://www.ibo.org/globalassets/publications/ib-research/jeff-thompson-award-mcintosh-final-report-en.pdf

12. Carroll, P., Child. S. F. J., & Darlington, E. (2015). Assessing active citizenship: An international perspective. *Research Matters, 19*, 14–19. https://www.cambridgeassessment.org.uk/Images/465777-assessing-active-citizenship-an-international-perspective.pdf

13. National Assessment of Educational Progress (NAEP). (2010). *NAEP questions tool*. http://nces.ed.gov/nationsreportcard/ITMRLSX/

14. Duke of Edinburgh's Award (DofE). (n.d.) *About the DofE*. https://www.dofe.org/about/

15. Ibid.

16. Duke of Edinburgh's International Award Foundation. (n.d.). *Assessor's guidance notes*. https://www.ttsonline.net/Uploads/documents/Duke%20of%20Edinburgh/Gold.pdf

17. Duke of Edinburgh's International Award Foundation. (2019). *A summary of research to date into the Duke of Edinburgh's International Award*. https://intaward.org/wp-content/uploads/2019/12/Summary-of-Research-to-Date-into-the-Award_V6_-August-2019.pdf

18. Richardson, M. (2010). Assessing the assessment of citizenship. *Research Papers in Education, 24*(4), 457–478.

19. UNESCO. (1996). *Learning: The treasure within*. https://unesdoc.unesco.org/ark:/48223/pf0000109590/PDF/109590engo.pdf.multi

20. Suto. (2013). op. cit.

CHAPTER 10

1. Hamann, K., Warneken, F., Greenberg, J., & Tomasello, M. (2011). Collaboration encourages equal sharing in children but not in chimpanzees. *Nature, 476*, 328–331. https://doi.org/10.1038/nature10278

2. Melis, A. P. (2013). The evolutionary roots of human collaboration: Coordination and sharing of resources. *Annals of the New York Academy of Sciences, 1299*(1), 68–76. https://doi.org/10.1111/nyas.12263

3. Kuhn, D. (2015). Thinking together and alone. *Educational Researcher, 44*(1), 46–53.
4. Partnership for 21st Century Learning. (2015). *Battelle for Kids.* http://www.p21.org/
5. Organisation for Economic Co-operation and Development (OECD). (2009). *Assessment for learning: Formative assessment.* Centre for Educational Research and Innovation, OECD.
6. Child, S. F. J., & Shaw, S. D. (2018). Towards an operational framework for establishing and assessing collaborative interactions. *Research Papers in Education.* https://doi.org/10.1080/02671522.2018.1424928
7. Child, S. F. J., & Shaw, S.D. (2016). Collaboration in the 21st century: Implications for assessment. *Research Matters, 22,* 17–22.
8. Shaw, S. D., & Child, S. F. J. (2017). Utilising technology in the assessment of collaboration: A critique of PISA's collaborative problem-solving tasks. *Research Matters, 24,* 17–22.
9. Siemon, J., Scholkmann, A., & Bloom, K.-D. *(2015, September 7–11).* '*Time on task' in collaborative learning: Influence of learning goal motivation and group composition* [Paper presentation]. European Conference for Education Research, Budapest.
10. Organisation for Economic Co-operation and Development (OECD). (2017). *Programme for International Student Assessment (PISA) 2015: Draft collaborative problem solving framework.* http://www.oecd.org/pisa/pisaproducts/Draft%20PISA%202015%20Collaborative%20Problem%20Solving%20Framework%20.pdf
11. Ibid. (p. 6)
12. Roschelle, J., & Teasley, S. D. (1995). The construction of shared knowledge in collaborative problem-solving. In C.E. O'Malley (Ed.), *Computer-supported collaborative learning* (pp. 69–97). Springer-Verlag.
13. Child & Shaw. (2016). op. cit.
14. Child & Shaw. (2018). op. cit.
15. Webb, N. M. (1991). Task-related verbal interaction and mathematics learning in small groups. *Journal for Research in Mathematics Education, 22*(5): 366–389.
16. Binkley, M., Erstad, O., Herman, J., Raizen, S., Ripley, M., & Rumble, M. (2010). *Defining 21st century skills* [Draft White Paper]. Learning and Technology World Forum.
17. Judd, T., Kennedy, G., & Cropper, S. (2010). Using wikis for collaborative learning: Assessing collaboration through contribution. *Australasian Journal of Educational Technology, 26*(3), 341–354.
18. Kreijns, K., Kirschner, P.A., & Vermeulen, M. (2013). Social aspects of CSCL environments: A research framework. *Educational Psychologist, 48*(4), 229–242.
19. Salomon, G., & Globerson, T. (1989). When teams do not function the way they ought to. *International Journal of Educational Research, 13*(1), 89–100.
20. Child & Shaw. (2016). op. cit.
21. Bossert, S. T. (1988). Cooperative activities in the classroom. *Review of Research in Education, 15,* 225–250.

CHAPTER 11

1. Gasser, N. (2019). *Why you like it: The science and culture of musical taste.* Flatiron Books.
2. Levitin, D. (2007). *This is your brain on music: Understanding a human obsession.* Atlantic Books. (p. 246)
3. Ibid. (p. 234)
4. Welsh Government. (2020). *Area of learning and expertise: Expressive arts.* https://hwb.gov.wales/curriculum-for-wales/expressive-arts

5. Cambridge Assessment. (2018). *Developing the Cambridge learner attributes*. https://www.cambridgeinternational.org/Images/417069-developing-the-cambridge-learner-attributes-.pdf (p. 69)
6. Cambridge Assessment. (2019). *Syllabus: Cambridge International AS & A level art & design 9479*. https://www.cambridgeinternational.org/Images/557248-2022-2024-syllabus.pdf
7. International Baccalaureate Organization (IBO). (2017). *International Baccalaureate Diploma Programme subject brief – The arts: Film*. https://ibo.org/contentassets/5895a05412144fe890312bad52b17044/film-sl-hl-2017-en.pdf
8. AQA. (2020). *GCSE drama 8261: Specification at a glance*. https://www.aqa.org.uk/subjects/drama/gcse/drama-8261/specification-at-a-glance
9. Queensland Curriculum and Assessment Authority (QCAA). (2019). *Dance: General senior syllabus*. https://www.qcaa.qld.edu.au/downloads/senior-qce/syllabuses/snr_dance_19_syll.pdf
10. Ellis, S., & Barrs, M. (2008). The assessment of creative learning. In J. Sefton-Green (Ed.), *Creative learning*. Arts Council England. https://www.creativitycultureeducation.org//wp-content/uploads/2018/10/creative-learning-booklet-26-233.pdf
11. Boughton, D. (2013). Assessment of performance in the visual arts: What, how, and why. In A. Kárpáti & E. Gaul. (Eds.), *From child art to visual language of youth: New models and tools for assessment of learning and creation in art education* (pp. 1–22). Intellect Press. (p. 1)
12. Schön, D. A. (1987). *Educating the reflective practitioner: Toward a new design for teaching and learning in the professions*. Jossey-Bass. (p. 93)
13. Beattie, D. K. (1997). *Assessment in art education*. Davis Publications.
14. Boughton. (2013). op. cit. (p. 7)
15. See, for example: Boughton. (2013). op. cit.; Ellis & Barrs. (2008). op. cit.
16. Koffka, K. (1935). *Principles of gestalt psychology*. Harcourt, Brace. (p. 176)
17. Abbotts, L. (2020). In conversation with author, August 2020.
18. Ibid.
19. Ibid.
20. Dan. (2006) *How to judge art: Five qualities you can critique whether you're an artist or not*. https://emptyeasel.com/2006/11/18/how-to-judge-art-five-qualities-you-can-critique/
21. Ibid.
22. University of Wisconsin–Green Bay. (1994). *Art criticism and formal analysis outline*. http://www.uwgb.edu/malloyk/art_criticism_and_formal_analysi.htm

CHAPTER 12

1. BusinessBalls. (n.d.). *Conscious competence learning model*. https://www.businessballs.com/self-awareness/conscious-competence-learning-model/
2. IAM RoadSmart (n.d.). *IAM RoadSmart*. https://www.iamroadsmart.com
3. Dweck, C. S. (2006). *Mindset: The new psychology of success*. Random House.
4. Folioano, F., Rolfe, H. Buzzeo, J., Runge, J., & Wilkinson, D. (2019). *Changing mindsets: Effectiveness trial*. https://www.niesr.ac.uk/sites/default/files/publications/Changing%20Mindsets_0.pdf
5. Syed, M. (2018). *You are awesome*. Wren & Rook.
6. Evidence Based Education. (2020). *Great teaching toolkit: Evidence review*. https://www.cambridgeinternational.org/support-and-training-for-schools/teaching-cambridge-at-your-school/great-teaching-toolkit/ (p. 6)
7. Ibid. (p. 30)

8. Black, P., & Wiliam, D. (1998). *Assessment and classroom learning: Assessment in education.* Routledge.
9. Boaler, J. (2015). *The elephant in the classroom.* Souvenir Press. (p. 85)
10. Black, P., & Wiliam, D. (2009). Developing the theory of formative assessment. *Educational Assessment, Evaluation and Accountability, 21*(1), 5–31. https://doi.org/10.1007/s11092-008-9068-5
11. Cambridge Assessment International Education. (2015). *Getting started with assessment for learning.* https://cambridge-community.org.uk/professional-development/gswafl/index.html
12. William, D. (2014, April). *Formative assessment and contingency in the regulation of learning processes* [Paper presentation]. Annual Meeting of American Educational Research Association. Philadelphia, PA. http://www.dylanwiliam.org/Dylan_Wiliams_website/Papers_files/Formative%20assessment%20and%20contingency%20in%20the%20regulation%20of%20learning%20processes%20%28AERA%202014%29.docx
13. James, M. (1998). *Using assessment for school improvement.* Heinemann.
14. Luxmoore, N. (2013). *School counsellors working with young people and staff: A whole-school approach.* Jessica Kingsley. (p. 59)
15. National Forum for the Enhancement of Teaching and Learning in Higher Education. (2017). *Expanding our understanding of assessment and feedback in Irish higher education.* https://www.teachingandlearning.ie/publication/expanding-our-understanding-of-assessment-and-feedback-in-irish-higher-education/
16. Black. & Wiliam. (1998). op. cit.
17. Cambridge Assessment International Education. (2015). *Getting started with metacognition.* https://cambridge-community.org.uk/professional-development/gswmeta/index.html
18. Zimmerman, B. J. (2002). Becoming a self-regulated learner: An overview. *Theory into Practice, 41*(2), 64–70.
19. Education Endowment Foundation (EEF). (2018). *Metacognition and self-regulated learning.* https://educationendowmentfoundation.org.uk/tools/guidance-reports/metacognition-and-self-regulated-learning/ (p. 9)
20. Boaler. (2015). op. cit. (p. 142)
21. Perkins, D. (1992). *Smart schools: Better thinking and learning for every child.* Free Press.
22. Cambridge Assessment International Education. (n.d.). *Getting started with metacognition.* https://cambridge-community.org.uk/professional-development/gswmeta/index.html
23. Smith, A. (2017). *Tips for effective exam preparation.* https://blog.cambridgeinternational.org/tips-for-effective-exam-preparation/
24. Assessment for Learning at King's. (n.d.). *Exam wrappers.* https://blogs.kcl.ac.uk/aflkings/students-directing-their-own-learning/exam-wrappers/
25. University of Sheffield. (n.d.). *Exam technique.* https://www.sheffield.ac.uk/ssid/301/study-skills/assessment/exam-techniques

CHAPTER 13

1. World Health Organization (WHO). (2021). *Mental health and substance use.* https://www.who.int/mental_health/en/
2. Boyd-MacMillan, E., & DeMarinis, V. (2020). *Learning passport: Curriculum framework (IC-ADAPT SEL high level programme design).* Cambridge University Press.
3. Harold, G. (2020). *Profile: Gordon Harold – Cambridge's new professor of the psychology of education and mental health.* https://www.educ.cam.ac.uk/facultyweb_content/news/content/profile-gordon-harold

4. Ofqual. (2020). *A review of the literature concerning anxiety for educational assessments.* Crown Copyright. (p. 7). The first half of this chapter draws on Ofqual's comprehensive literature review.
5. Ofqual. (2019). *Coping with exam pressure: A guide for students.* Crown Copyright.
6. Ofqual. (2020). op. cit. (pp. 19–20, 25)
7. Putwain, D. W. (2008). Deconstructing test anxiety. *Emotional and Behavioural Difficulties, 13*(2), 141–155.
8. Ofqual. (2020). op. cit. (pp. 22–32)
9. Ibid. (pp. 33–39)
10. Von der Embse, N., Jester, D., Roy, D., & Post, J. (2018). Test anxiety effects, predictors, and correlates: A 30-year meta-analytic review. *Journal of Affective Disorders, 227,* 483–493.
11. Putwain, D. W., Daly, A. L., Chamberlain, S., & Sadreddini, S. (2015). Academically buoyant students are less anxious about and perform better in high-stakes examinations. *British Journal of Educational Psychology, 85,* 247–263.
12. Roome, T. (2018). *Exam stress experienced by GCSE students in a mainstream secondary school: Perceptions of the effects on wellbeing and performance* [Unpublished doctoral thesis]. University of Birmingham.
13. Blakemore, S.-J. (2018). *Inventing ourselves: The secret life of the teenage brain.* Black Swan.
14. Ofqual. (2020). op. cit. (p. 24)
15. Hutchings, M. (2015). *Exam factories: The impact of accountability measures on children and young people.* National Union of Teachers.
16. Ofqual. (2020). op. cit. (p. 27)
17. Ibid. (p. 26)
18. McLeod, C. In conversation with author, August 2020.
19. Walker, M. (2017). *Why we sleep.* Penguin. (pp. 114–115)
20. Whitmore, J. (2017). *Coaching for performance.* Nicholas Brearley Publishing.
21. Burke, A., & Hawkins, K. In conversation with author, August 2020.
22. Ibid.
23. BBC. *Exams: How to deal with exam stress.* https://www.bbc.co.uk/bitesize/articles/zsvcqhv
24. Ibid.
25. Gallwey, T. (1974). *The inner game of tennis.* Random House.

CHAPTER 14

1. Blume, H. (1998). Neurodiversity: On the neurological underpinnings of geekdom. *The Atlantic.* https://www.theatlantic.com/magazine/archive/1998/09/neurodiversity/305909/
2. Masataka, N. (2017). Implications of the idea of neurodiversity for understanding the origins of developmental disorders. *Physics of Life Review, 20,* 85–108.
3. UNESCO. (2020). *Global education monitoring report: Inclusion and education: ALL MEANS ALL.* UNESCO.
4. Cambridge Assessment International Education. (2020). *Education brief: Inclusive education.* https://www.cambridgeinternational.org/Images/599369-education-brief-inclusive-education.pdf
5. Ofqual. (2019). *Access arrangements for GCSE, AS and A level 2018 to 2019 academic year.* Crown Copyright. (p. 2)
6. Waterfield, J., & West, B. (2006). *Inclusive assessment in higher education: A resource for change.* University of Plymouth.

7. Woods, K., James, A., & Hipkiss, A. (2018). Best practice in access arrangements made for England's General Certificates of Secondary Education (GCSEs): Where are we 10 years on? *British Journal of Special Education, 45*(2). https://doi.org/10.1111/1467-8578.12221

8. Ofqual. (2019). op. cit. (p. 5)

9. Cambridge Assessment International Education. (2019). *Cambridge handbook 2020 (international)*. Cambridge Assessment.

10. University of Worcester. (2004). *Strategies for creating inclusive programmes of study (SCIPS)*. https://scips.worc.ac.uk/?sfid=1298&_sft_key-skill-category=assessment

11. Cambridge Assessment International Education. (2017). *Code of practice*. UCLES. (Aim 2.4)

12. Ibid.

13. Council of Europe. (n.d.). *The CEFR levels*. https://www.coe.int/en/web/common-european-framework-reference-languages/level-descriptions

14. Shaw, S. D. (2020). Achieving in content through language: Towards a CEFR descriptor scale for academic language proficiency. In M. DeBoer. & D. Leontjev (Eds.), *Assessment and learning in content and language integrated learning (CLIL) classrooms: Approaches and conceptualisations* (pp. 29–56). Springer.

15. Imam, H., & Shaw, S. D. (2011). *International learning and assessment through the medium of English*. [Poster presentation].

16. UNESCO. (2020). op. cit. (p. 132)

17. Waterfield, J., & West, B. (2006). *Inclusive assessment in higher education: A resource for change*. University of Plymouth.

18. Ibid. (p. 20)

19. Meyer, A., Rose, D., & Gordon D. (2013). *Universal Design for Learning: Theory and practice*. CAST.

20. Eaton, R., & Osborne, A. (2018). *Patterns beyond labels model of inclusive practice*. University of Bath.

21. Plymouth University. (2016). *Inclusive assessment: Good practice guide*. https://www.plymouth.ac.uk/uploads/production/document/path/2/2516/Good_practice_inclusive_assessment_updated_May_2016.pdf

22. National Forum for the Enhancement of Teaching and Learning in Higher Education. (2017). *Assessment of/for/as learning*. https://www.teachingandlearning.ie/our-priorities/student-success/assessment-of-for-as-learning/#!/Principles

23. Plymouth University. (2014). *7 steps to inclusive assessment*. https://www.plymouth.ac.uk/uploads/production/document/path/2/2401/7_Steps_to_Inclusive_Assessment.pdf

24. Plymouth University. (n.d.). *Inclusive assessment*. https://www.plymouth.ac.uk/about-us/teaching-and-learning/inclusivity/inclusive-assessment

25. Waterfield & West. (2006). op. cit. (p. 154)

26. Osborne, A. In conversation with author, July–August 2020.

27. Arizona State University. (2016). *Integrating technology with Bloom's taxonomy*. https://teachonline.asu.edu/2016/05/integrating-technology-blooms-taxonomy/

28. Plymouth University. (2016). op. cit. (p. 10)

29. Mueller, J. (2016). *What is authentic assessment?* http://jfmueller.faculty.noctrl.edu/toolbox/whatisit.htm

30. National Forum for the Enhancement of Teaching and Learning in Higher Education. (2017). *Authentic assessment in Irish higher education*. https://www.teachingandlearning.ie/publication/authentic-assessment-in-irish-higher-education/

31. UNESCO. (2020). op. cit. (p. 136)

CHAPTER 15

1. Hughes, C. (2020). COVID-19 and the opportunity to design a more mindful approach to learning. *Prospects, 49,* 69–72. https://doi.org/10.1007/s11125-020-09480-3

2. Robinson, K. (2006). *Do Schools Kill Creativity?* https://www.ted.com/talks/sir_ken_robinson_do_schools_kill_creativity?language=en

3. Association of School and College Leaders (ASCL). (2019). *The forgotten third: Final report of the Commission of Inquiry.* https://www.ascl.org.uk/ASCL/media/ASCL/Our%20view/Campaigns/The-Forgotten-Third_full-report.pdf

4. Lucas, B., Hyman, P., & McConville, A. (2020, September 27). 3 reasons GCSEs need to change and 3 alternatives. *Times Educational Supplement.* https://www.tes.com/news/gcses-2021-change-alternatives

5. Hughes, C. In conversation with author, October 2020.

6. Blakemore, S.-J. (2018). *Inventing ourselves: The secret life of the teenage brain.* Black Swan. (p. 188)

7. Elmore, R. (2019). The future of learning and the future of assessment. *ECNU Review of Education, 2*(3), 328–341. https://doi.org/10.1177/2096531119878962 (p. 331)

8. Ibid. (p. 333)

9. AQA. (2015). *The future of assessment: 2025 and beyond.* https://filestore.aqa.org.uk/content/about-us/AQA-THE-FUTURE-OF-ASSESSMENT.PDF

10. Boud, D., & Associates. (2010). *Assessment 2020: Seven propositions for assessment reform in higher education.* https://ltr.edu.au/resources/Assessment%202020_final.pdf

11. Tierney, S. (2020, October 13). Is it time to reboot our entire exams system? *Times Educational Supplement.* https://www.tes.com/news/it-time-reboot-our-entire-exams-system

12. Wiliam, D. (2020). *Assessment for learning in a changing world* [Paper presentation]. Cambridge Assessment International Education.

13. Béguin, A., & Wood, A. (2015). Using exam results to inform teaching and accountability. In D. Bassett (Ed.), *The future of assessment: 2025 and beyond.* AQA. (p. 48)

14. JISC. (2020). *The future of assessment: Five principles, five targets for 2025.* https://repository.jisc.ac.uk/7733/1/the-future-of-assessment-report.pdf (p. 10)

15. Smith, M. E. (2014). *Results of the consultation on revised A level subject content.* https://assets.publishing.service.gov.uk/government/uploads/system/uploads/attachment_data/file/301060/Post-consultation_report_on_A_levels.pdf

16. Gulikers, J. (2006). *Authenticity is in the eye of the beholder: Beliefs and perceptions of authentic assessment and the influence on student learning.* Interuniversity Center for Educational Research, Open-Universiteit-Nederland.

17. Huddleston, P. (2015). How should we assess vocational and practical learning? In D. Bassett (Ed.), *The future of assessment: 2025 and beyond.* AQA. (p. 28)

18. Bramley, T., & Crisp, V. (2019). Spoilt for choice? Issues around the use and comparability of optional exam questions. *Assessment in Education: Principles, Policy & Practice, 26*(1), 75–90. https://doi.org/10.1080/0969594X.2017.1287662

19. Puentedura, R. (2010). *SAMR and TPCK: Intro to advanced practice.* http://hippasus.com/resources/sweden2010/SAMR_TPCK_IntroToAdvancedPractice.pdf

20. Brown, G. T. L. (2017). The future of assessment as a human and social endeavor: Addressing the inconvenient truth of error. *Frontiers in Education: Assessment, Testing and Applied Measurement, 2*(3). https://doi.org/10.3389/feduc.2017.00003

21. JISC. (2020). *The future of assessment: Five principles, five targets for 2025.* https://repository.jisc.ac.uk/7733/1/the-future-of-assessment-report.pdf (p. 23)

INDEX

Made in the USA
Monee, IL
30 May 2023

34949911R00111